HOME PLATES

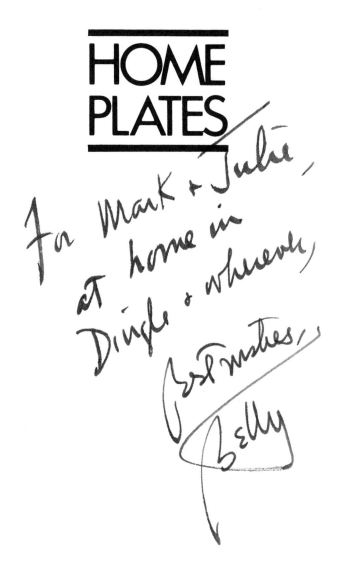

For Mark + Julie,
at home in
Dingle + wherever,
Best wishes,
Betty

ALSO BY BETTY FUSSELL

Masters of American Cookery
I Hear America Cooking
Eating In
Food in Good Season

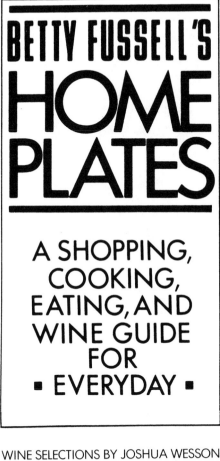

BETTY FUSSELL'S HOME PLATES

A SHOPPING, COOKING, EATING, AND WINE GUIDE FOR ▪ EVERYDAY ▪

WINE SELECTIONS BY JOSHUA WESSON
AND DAVID ROSENGARTEN

DUTTON 〰 NEW YORK

DUTTON
Published by the Penguin Group
Penguin Books USA Inc., 375 Hudson Street,
New York, New York 10014, U.S.A.
Penguin Books Ltd, 27 Wrights Lane,
London W8 5TZ, England
Penguin Books Australia Ltd, Ringwood,
Victoria, Australia
Penguin Books Canada Ltd, 2801 John Street,
Markham, Ontario, Canada L3R 1B4
Penguin Books (N.Z.) Ltd, 182–190 Wairau Road,
Auckland 10, New Zealand

Penguin Books Ltd, Registered Offices:
Harmondsworth, Middlesex, England

First published by Dutton, an imprint of Penguin Books
USA Inc.

First printing, July, 1990
10 9 8 7 6 5 4 3 2 1

Library of Congress Cataloging-in-Publication Data

Fussell, Betty Harper.
    Betty Fussell's home plates: a shopping, cooking,
eating & wine guide for everyday / Betty Fussell; wine
selections by Joshua Wesson and David Rosengarten. —
1st ed.
        p.   cm.
    ISBN 0-525-24861-7
    1. Cookery.   I. Title.   II. Title: Home plates.
TX714.F87   1990
641.5 — dc20   89-37894
                    CIP

Printed in the United States of America
Designed by Margo D. Barooshian

ACKNOWLEDGMENTS

Thanks to Leah Holzel for testing and tasting—again and again. Thanks to Carole DeSanti, Mary Wagstaff, and Amanda Vaill for publishing the results. And thanks to my friends, but especially Matthew Culligan, for bravery under constant culinary fire.

CONTENTS

PASTA

SHELLFISH

FISH

BIRDS

MEATS

MISCELLANEOUS

COMPANIONS

AFTERWARDS

HOME
PLATES

INTRODUCTION

Thank God for eating out. It makes eating in such a pleasure. Eating out is one of those grim urban necessities, like jammed subways, maniacal cab drivers, ear-splitting sirens, hostile beggars, and friendly muggers. Eating in is a moment set apart, a moment of peace and security, of candlelight and fine wines that you can afford because they're not triply marked up, a moment that you control from beginning to end. A moment for the two of you . . . whether it's you and another, or you and yourself. This book is designed to help both of you make the most of it—home free, home safe.

Since junk time is more valuable than junk bonds to urbanites on the run, this book is physically designed to make shopping and cooking as fast as possible so that eating may be as leisurely as possible. With this guide in hand, purse, or pocket, you can improvise shopping as easily as cooking. Make a note of major ingredients—the ones that you might have to shop for or that distinguish a particular dish—so that you can square what the market has with what the dish requires. If the shrimp in the store looks suspect, forget Charred Shrimp Poblano and move on to Roasted Garlic Cod. If the pears are ripe, forget Gingered Figs and think Pernod Pears.

The minor ingredients used in these recipes are staples you should keep in your kitchen: flour, sugar, extra-virgin olive oil, unsalted butter, good red and white wine vinegars, onions, garlic, lemons, sea salt, pepper in a grinder, and dry spices in small quantities kept away from heat and light. In addition, the recipes in this book draw on a range of flavorings we've learned to enjoy from the ongoing ethnic hodgepodge of our cities: Chinese, Thai, Japanese, Italian, Latin American. Today, a well-stocked kitchen will also include soy sauce, cumin seeds, gingerroot (fresh or frozen), jalapeño peppers or other fresh hot chili peppers, balsamic vinegar, fresh cilantro. *Fresh* is the key word in the recipes that follow: black pepper, as well as cumin, coriander, and nutmeg are always freshly ground. Parsley and cilantro are always market-fresh. Lime, lemon, and orange juices are always freshly squeezed.

Wise shoppers go for the best and waste nothing. Good fresh pasta has become a staple, thank God, in urban markets, but it's good to keep on hand a couple of dried pastas of good brands like Ronzoni or San Giorgio. It's also wise to keep anchovy paste, olives, and good Parmesan to grate at the last moment so that you can improvise a meal without having to plan or shop. More and more health-minded shoppers are substituting extra-virgin olive oil for butter, yogurt for cream, chicken and fish for red meats, and vegetable purée sauces for flour and eggs. Sophisticated shoppers are learning that when a fine triple-cream cheese like mascarpone is called for, another triple-cream can be substituted, but that processed commercial stuff designed for eternal shelf life just won't do.

For cooking you need only one pot—a wok—and one knife: a Chinese cleaver kept sharp with a nifty, easy sharpener like Chantry. Of course you can use whatever pots and knives you've got, but the Chinese have been at this for a few thousand years and it shows. What America contributed was the blender, without which you can forget quick purées. With a blender, a food processor is not a necessity, but when time is money, it sure helps. The processor can do what the blender can't in the way of a kinder and gentler mixing, beating, chopping, and grinding. Countertop toaster or convection ovens are a luxury, but useful for small-quantity cooking. Microwaves are good for zapping freezer foods or baked potatoes, but otherwise their ovens just take up space. I'd rather have a wok with a lid. Quantities in these recipes are designed for two. You can double them for four, or triple them for six. Of course you can halve a recipe to cook for one, but it's harder to shop for one. Better to follow the recipe as is and keep leftovers for new combinations the next day.

Leftovers are one of the great advantages of eating in. My best meals are often icebox meals, concocted with a little imagination and a lot of bravura from whatever odd foods tumble out from refrigerator shelves. Many dishes benefit from a sleepover—dishes like chowders, pâtés, many sauces, and purées. Some dishes, like pasta, change character the morning after to surprise and delight when they are given a slow baking in the oven or a quick crisping in a skillet.

As food costs soar, so does our need for thrift, thrift, Horatio. Eating in, we can maximize our food investment. Maddeningly small dabs of sauce, soup, fresh or cooked vegetables, scraps of bones and herbs, can go into freezer bags to later enrich a sauce, soup, stew, stockpot, etc. Leftover wine can go into our red or white vinegar bottles.

These recipes are designed, as much as possible, to make one-dish meals for those as thrifty of time as of money. Although the book is structured on the order of a three-course meal, from Starters to Afterwards, almost any of the dishes can become a satisfying meal in itself. All a soup requires is a crusty bread or some good crackers to make a balanced meal. All a fruit dessert requires is some shortbread or an oatmeal muffin to turn an afterthought into a main dish. On a hot day, I've made a lunch of Jalapeño-Lime Ice. With eating, as with other appetites, the key to satisaction is not how much or how many or how varied, but how good.

For those times when you want diversity in a meal, I've suggested for each dish other foods or dishes that make natural couplings, without forgetting that excitement comes from unexpected combinations. I've also suggested a variant for each recipe to encourage the notion that recipes are no more than brief scenarios, notations, memos to help the production of a dish or meal. They are meaningless until put into action by the cook with his own taste, temperament, and technique, not to mention whim. Eating in, yours is the only taste that counts, yours the only pleasure. You're the king of the kitchen, so go for it.

Eating in, we can explore a range of wines prohibitive when eating out. Fortunately, wine experts Joshua Wesson and David Rosengarten contributed wine suggestions, a pair of them for each dish, to help us choose by wallet and taste among the myriad labels now flooding our cities from places as unlikely as Yugoslavia and as local as Long Island.

For me, the real pleasure of eating in is cooking in, whether I'm alone or doubled. Cooking, even more than eating, is the best way to get the whole heady, sensuous, sexy feel of the textures, flavors, and smells of oysters dripping curry butter, of chickens soothed by coconut and refreshed by lemon grass, of purple-skinned eggplant stir-fried with apples, of creamy chocolate zinged by hot chili. The choice is endless and the choice is all mine—and yours.

After a long day's work, what do I look forward to? A long night's wait elbow-to-belly in a packed restaurant bar, ear drums shattered by the din of compulsory conviviality, wallet depleted and tongue shriveled by the touted house wine? No, fellow eater. I dream of a quick run through my local Korean grocer, the opening of a cold Oregon Chardonnay, the speedy tossing together of tender fettuccine with orange juice and toasted almonds (just wait 'til you try that one), the slow relishing of a moment I have created that redeems the long day, a moment to share with another, or another part of myself—savoring together the pleasure and comfort of home plates.

STARTERS

CHILI-CARROT SOUP ♦ RED
PEPPER–GARLIC SOUP ♦ CORN &
SORREL SOUP ♦ DAIKON &
MINT SOUP ♦ ORANGE-CRANBERRY
SOUP ♦ WILD MUSHROOM PÂTÉ
♦ SMOKED SALMON & MASCARPONE
TERRINE ♦ CHINESE
SHRIMP-IN-THE-SHELL ♦ WOK-
SMOKED TROUT ♦ SMOKED
HADDOCK BRANDADE ♦ ROASTED
OYSTERS WITH CURRY BUTTER

CHILI-CARROT SOUP

1 tablespoon butter or olive oil
¼ pound carrots, sliced
1 small onion, sliced
½ jalapeño pepper, seeded and minced
2 slices gingerroot, minced
2 cups hot chicken stock
½ cup fresh orange juice
Salt and black pepper to taste
1 tablespoon chopped fresh cilantro for garnish

Heat butter or oil and gently sauté carrots, onion, jalapeño pepper, and ginger until softened, about 5 minutes. Add stock, cover pan, and simmer 10 minutes, or until vegetables are fork-tender. Purée mixture in a blender and return liquid to pan. Add orange juice, taste and adjust seasoning, and bring to the simmer. If soup is too thick, add more stock. Garnish with cilantro.

Serve hot or cold, with papadums or toasted bialis.

◆ Instead of orange juice, add a large ripe tomato, seeded and chopped, to the vegetables in the sauté pan. Or simply add ½ cup tomato juice. To turn soup into a carrot purée for a vegetable garnish, double the amount of carrots and diminish the total liquid to 1 cup: ¾ cup stock, ¼ cup orange juice.

RED PEPPER–
GARLIC SOUP

2 tablespoons olive oil
2 sweet red peppers, seeded and chopped
10 cloves garlic, mashed
1 cup chicken or fish stock
½ to 1 teaspoon balsamic vinegar
Salt and black pepper to taste
4 fresh sage leaves for garnish

Heat oil and sauté peppers and garlic over moderately high heat for 1 or 2 minutes. Add stock, bring to the boil, cover, and simmer gently for about 15 minutes or until vegetables are soft. Purée vegetables with the liquid in a blender. Add vinegar and seasoning. Garnish soup with sage.

Serve with a crusty French or Italian loaf or with Roast Potato Chips and an Orange-Onion-Basil Salad with Tahini Dressing.

◆   Change the soup to a sauce by using only ¼ cup liquid, or just enough to make a purée. This sauce is particularly good on linguine, spaghettini, or a grilled fish.

CORN & SORREL SOUP

1 tablespoon butter or olive oil
1½ cups sorrel leaves, packed
3 cups chicken stock
2 ears sweet corn, kernels cut off, about 2 cups
Salt and black pepper to taste
Fresh basil leaves or dill for garnish

Heat butter or oil, add sorrel leaves and wilt over low heat. Add stock and bring liquid to the boil. Put corn kernels in a blender, add sorrel soup, and purée (easier to do in 2 batches). Add seasoning. Garnish bowls with basil, dill, or other fresh herbs. This soup is good hot or cold.

Serve with a hefty salad like Hot Potato Salad with Mussels or Hot Bacon & Egg Salad.

♦ Instead of sorrel, use tender greens such as mustard, turnip, or dandelion. For a creamier texture, use 2½ cups stock and 1½ cup buttermilk or half-and-half.

DAIKON & MINT SOUP

1 tablespoon olive oil
¾ cup chopped onion
¾ cup peeled and chopped daikon
1½ cups chicken stock
¾ cup plain yogurt
3 tablespoons chopped fresh mint leaves
Salt and black pepper to taste

Heat oil and sauté onion and daikon for 2 or 3 minutes, or until softened. Add stock, bring to a boil, then purée mixture in a blender. Add yogurt and half of the mint, blend, and taste and adjust seasoning. Pour soup into bowls and garnish with remaining mint leaves. Good hot or cold.

Make a full meal with a bowl of Red Lentils or an Onion-Cheese Soufflé.

♦ Steamed daikon is delicate and delicious. Dice or cut it lengthwise into strips like carrot strips, then steam for 3 or 4 minutes. Toss in melted butter or mix with yogurt flavored with sautéed onion and chopped mint.

ORANGE-CRANBERRY SOUP

1½ tablespoons butter
3 green onions, chopped
1½ cups chicken broth
¾ cup cranberries
2 oranges
2 tablespoons dry sherry

Heat butter and sauté onions for 2 or 3 minutes, until soft. Add broth and cranberries, bring to the simmer, and cook gently for 5 to 6 minutes, until cranberries pop. Purée mixture in a blender. Cut the oranges in half. Cut 2 thin slices from 1 of the halves for garnish and squeeze remaining oranges for juice to get ¾ cup. Add juice and sherry to cranberry purée. If serving soup hot, reheat liquid gently for a moment or two. Otherwise, chill liquid until ready for use. Garnish each bowl with a slice of orange.

Serve as a starter for a dish of Turkey Scallopini or for grilled quail or roast chicken.

♦ Use beets instead of cranberries for a darker red and slightly sweeter soup. Balance the sweetness of beets by adding a little lemon juice or a dash of sherry vinegar instead of dry sherry.

WILD MUSHROOM PÂTÉ

½ pound wild mushrooms (shiitake, oyster,
    morel, chanterelle)
4 tablespoons butter
1 green onion with top, chopped
2 tablespoons hazelnuts, skins on, chopped fine
½ teaspoon Worcestershire sauce
1 to 2 tablespoons brandy
Salt and black and cayenne peppers to taste

Cut off the root end of the mushroom stems if they are sandy and discard. Slice mushrooms and their stems. Heat butter in a large sauté pan over high heat. Brown mushrooms and onion about 4 minutes. Add chopped nuts and brown 1 minute. Lower heat and cook for 2 more minutes to release mushroom juices. Put mixture in a food processor, add Worcestershire, brandy, and seasonings, and pulse until mixture is finely chopped. Pack pâté into a pottery bowl for serving (keeps well refrigerated for about a week).

Serve on toast or in pita halves.

♦   Serve as a salad by piling mushroom mixture on a bed of arugula, watercress, or mixed garden greens. Or, surround the mushroom mixture with slices of smoked chicken or turkey breast, with sliced avocado, or spears of crisp asparagus.

SMOKED SALMON
& MASCARPONE TERRINE

¼ pound smoked salmon, about 6 thin slices
½ lemon
Black pepper to taste
½ pound mascarpone (or triple-cream cheese)
2 tablespoons fresh salmon caviar

Overlap 2 slices of smoked salmon in the middle of a piece of plastic wrap in order to make a small rectangle (about 4 inches × 2 inches). Squeeze on a bit of lemon juice, sprinkle with a grinding of black pepper, and spread with a third of the mascarpone. Repeat with remaining slices of salmon and mascarpone to make 2 more layers of salmon with mascarpone on top. Cover top with caviar. Wrap layered "loaf" in the plastic wrap and chill until ready to serve. Cut loaf in half, crosswise.

Serve with thin slices of buttered rye or whole wheat bread or with bagel chips. Or, use as a salad and surround with shredded radicchio or a circle of endive leaves.

◆ Make a pâté by puréeing the salmon in a food processor with the same ingredients, but use only half the amount of mascarpone and garnish with caviar.

CHINESE SHRIMP-
IN-THE-SHELL

¾ pound shrimp
1 teaspoon salt
½ teaspoon Szechuan peppercorns, ground
½ teaspoon sugar
1 tablespoon each of minced garlic and
*   gingerroot*
1 green onion, minced
1 small fresh red or green chili pepper, seeded
*   and minced*
1 cup peanut or vegetable oil

Rinse shrimp, then cut through the shell along outside edge, leaving the shell on. Blot shrimp dry with paper towels. Mix salt, Szechuan pepper, and sugar and set aside. Mix garlic, ginger, onion, and chili pepper and set aside. Heat oil in a wok or deep skillet until smoking hot. Add half the shrimp and fry for 1 minute, then remove with slotted spoon and drain on paper towels. Repeat with remaining shrimp. Discard oil but don't wipe out pan. Place wok over high heat. Add salt mixture and stir for a few seconds, then garlic mixture, then shrimp. Stir-fry for about 2 minutes, turning shrimp to coat on all sides. Serve hot or at room temperature.

Serve shrimp with Chinese Cabbage & Pink Grapefruit Slaw, Honeyed Golden Peppers, or Thai Papaya Salad.

◆   For a different flavor, use the same basic seasonings but smoke the shrimp (see following recipe). Place shrimp in a single layer over ¼ cup each of tea, brown sugar, and rice, mixed with chili pepper, garlic, ginger, and onion, and smoke for 5 minutes over high heat, then 15 minutes off heat with the lid still on.

WOK-SMOKED
TROUT

2 fresh brook trout
¼ cup each: *black tea leaves, brown rice, and
brown sugar*
*A few sprigs of fresh thyme (or 1 teaspoon dried
thyme)*
*A few sprigs of fresh rosemary (or 1 teaspoon
dried rosemary)*
*Fresh Italian parsley or cilantro and lemon
wedges for garnish*

Rinse trout and pat dry. Line a wok with heavy aluminum foil. In the center, mix tea leaves, rice, and sugar, and cover with herbs. Place a rack over the mixture. Line wok lid with foil and cover pan. Set over high heat for about 5 minutes. Remove lid, place trout on rack, leaving space between the 2 fish, then replace lid. Smoke over high heat for 5 minutes. Turn off heat and let wok sit, with lid on, for 15 minutes. Remove lid and serve hot or at room temperature. Garnish trout with fresh Italian parsley or cilantro and serve with a wedge of lemon.

Follow the trout with Gorgonzola Risotto.

◆ Instead of smoking trout, place trout in 2 tablespoons butter with rosemary and thyme in a sealed packet of aluminum foil. Steam in a 350°F. oven for 7 to 10 minutes.

SMOKED HADDOCK BRANDADE

½ pound smoked haddock (sable or whitefish)
1 clove garlic, minced
½ cup heavy cream
¼ cup olive oil
Pinch of ground nutmeg
Salt and black and cayenne peppers to taste
Lemon juice to taste

Skin and bone the fish. Put the fish and garlic into a food processor and process until well ground. Heat the cream and oil in separate pans. Add cream to mixture in processor and blend well. While processor is on, add oil slowly through the opening in lid and purée until oil is absorbed. Taste and season with spices and lemon juice.

Serve on toasted slices of French sourdough bread or put purée in the middle of a bowl of mashed potatoes. Brandade is rich in itself and can serve as a full meal with a green salad and a fruit dessert.

◆ Turn similar ingredients into a soup by flaking the fish instead of puréeing, and heating gently with sautéed diced onions and garlic in fish stock (or clam juice) enriched with milk or half-and-half.

ROASTED OYSTERS
WITH CURRY BUTTER

2 dozen oysters in the shell
6 tablespoons butter
½ teaspoon Madras Curry Powder
½ teaspoon minced gingerroot
1 teaspoon fresh lime juice
Salt and black pepper to taste

Preheat oven to 500°F. Crinkle aluminum foil in bottom of a large baking pan to make a nest for the oysters. Place oysters rounded side down in the foil, cover with a large sheet of foil, and seal edges. Roast for 6 to 9 minutes (depending on size), until shells open just enough to pry them apart.

Meanwhile melt butter in a small pan with curry and ginger. Remove pan from the heat and add lime juice. After oysters are roasted and have opened, remove top shells, spoon a little curry butter onto each oyster, season as desired, and serve oysters in their foil nest.

For a special occasion, follow oysters with Venison with Mustard Fruits, accompanied by a green salad. Finish the meal with Dried Apricot Fool.

◆   Roast oysters on an outside grill by covering them with a sheet of foil when coals are ready. Or you can poach shucked oysters in curry butter by melting butter with seasonings in a sauté pan, adding oysters, and gently simmering until their edges just begin to curl.

PASTA

PASTA WITH ROASTED PEANUTS ◆
MUSTARD-LEMON LINGUINE WITH
ASPARAGUS ◆ PENNE WITH
CHARRED VEGETABLES ◆ PASTA
WITH ANCHOVY, FENNEL &
FETA ◆ PASTA WITH BLACK BEANS
& SUN-DRIED TOMATOES ◆
FETTUCCINE WITH OYSTERS ◆
ORZO WITH PINE NUTS &
CURRANTS ◆ SWEET LEMON
NOODLES ◆ ORANGE-ALMOND
FETTUCCINE ◆ PASTA WITH
ARTICHOKES & OLIVES

PASTA WITH
ROASTED PEANUTS

1½ tablespoons olive oil
1 small onion, chopped
1 to 2 cloves garlic, minced
1 tomato, seeded and chopped
2 to 3 slices gingerroot, minced
Black and cayenne peppers to taste
1 tablespoon peanut butter
½ teaspoon soy sauce
½ cup chicken broth
⅓ pound dried pasta (farfalle, penne,
*   macaroni)*
⅓ cup roasted peanuts, chopped
3 or 4 sprigs fresh cilantro for garnish

Bring 3 quarts of water (with a tablespoon of salt and a teaspoon of olive oil) to a boil.

Prepare the sauce by heating oil in a skillet and sautéing onion and garlic 4 to 5 minutes, until softened. Add tomato, ginger, and black and cayenne peppers. Thin peanut butter with soy sauce and chicken broth and add to mixture in skillet. Bring liquid to the simmer, cover pan, and remove from heat.

Cook pasta in the boiling water, test after 3 or 4 minutes, and cook until *al dente*. Drain and toss pasta with sauce. Garnish with chopped peanuts and cilantro sprigs.

Serve hot or at room temperature with Chinese Cabbage & Pink Grapefruit Slaw, fresh green beans, or a mixed green salad.

◆ ˙ Use the same peanut sauce for a stir-fry dish of pork slivers, chunks of chicken, shrimp, or tofu, mixed with bean sprouts and fresh or dried hot chili pepper.

◇ With this dish, try an acidic wine with a touch of sweetness, like a QbA Riesling from the Mosel, or a light Riesling from Washington State.

MUSTARD-LEMON
LINGUINE WITH
ASPARAGUS

4 to 6 spears asparagus
2 tablespoons butter
1 tablespoon olive oil
1 to 1½ tablespoons Dijon mustard
1 cup heavy cream
Rind and juice of ½ lemon
⅓ pound dried linguine
Salt and black pepper to taste
Grated Parmesan cheese

Bring 3 quarts of water (with a tablespoon of salt and a teaspoon of oil) to a boil.

Bring about 1 cup of salted water to a boil in a skillet just large enough to hold the asparagus spears. Simmer asparagus 4 to 6 minutes (depending on size), until just fork-tender but still crisp. Remove spears but save liquid in a bowl.

Make sauce by heating butter and oil in the sauce pan. Beat in mustard and cream, and simmer for 3 or 4 minutes. Add lemon rind, juice, and seasoning, and keep warm while cooking the pasta.

Cook linguine in the boiling water, test after 3 or 4 minutes, and cook until *al dente*. Drain and toss pasta with sauce and asparagus. If sauce is too thick, add a little asparagus juice. Sprinkle with Parmesan cheese.

Serve with Sautéed Escarole and Chili Oranges.

◆ For a creamy sauce without cream, roast a dozen garlic cloves with their skins on in the butter and oil, enclosed in foil, at 350°F. for about 10 minutes (roasted garlic loses its edge and has a rich, nutty taste). Remove garlic and press flesh from the skins into the butter and oil. Put in a blender with the mustard, lemon, and ¼ cup white wine (or asparagus juice) and blend until smooth.

◇ Look for a light, fairly neutral white wine like an Italian Chardonnay or a white Bordeaux from the region of Entre-deux-Mers.

PENNE WITH
CHARRED VEGETABLES

1 small onion
½ sweet red pepper
½ small or Japanese eggplant
½ small zucchini
2 cloves garlic
1 tablespoon olive oil
⅓ pound penne (or other dried pasta)
Salt and black pepper to taste

Bring 3 quarts of water (with a tablespoon of salt and a teaspoon of oil) to the boil.

Cut onion in eighths. Cut halved red pepper in ½-inch strips. Cut halved eggplant and zucchini lengthwise into slices ¼ inch thick. Peel and slice the garlic.

Heat a wok or heavy skillet until very hot. Add the oil, then onion and red pepper. Turn vegetables to char on all sides, then remove to a warm platter. Add eggplant, zucchini, and garlic. Char vegetables as quickly as possible, turning to brown on both sides, then add to onion and peppers.

Cook pasta in boiling water, test after 3 or 4 minutes, and cook until *al dente*. Drain and mix with vegetables, seasoning to taste.

This is a hearty meal in itself. Follow with a light dessert like Gingered Figs.

♦   Anything charred this way is going to complement the blandness of pasta, so try different kinds of vegetables or small fish fillets, shrimp, or very thin strips of beef. Or, if you want more of a sauce, pureé some of the charred vegetables for a nice smoky taste.

◇   Light, fruity red wines, like Beaujolais and Dolcetta d'Alba, cozy right up to the blackened veggies in this dish.

PASTA WITH ANCHOVY, FENNEL & FETA

1 head fennel
1 tablespoon each of butter and olive oil
1 to 2 cloves garlic, minced
2 green onions with tops, chopped
6 to 8 anchovy fillets, plus 1 tablespoon of their
      oil (or 2 teaspoons anchovy paste, plus
      1 tablespoon olive oil)
⅓ pound spaghettini (or other dried pasta)
Black pepper to taste
⅓ cup crumbled feta cheese

Bring 3 quarts of water (with a tablespoon of salt and a teaspoon of oil) to a boil.

Cut off and discard the root end and stalky tops of the fennel, saving ¼ cup of the ferny leaves and several sprigs for garnish. Trim off any discolored areas on the outside layer of the fennel, then slice the head crosswise. Chop the reserved fennel leaves. Heat butter and oil and sauté fennel with garlic and onions about 2 to 3 minutes, until they are somewhat softened. Chop anchovies and add with their oil to fennel. Add black pepper and the chopped fennel leaves.

Cook pasta in the boiling water, test after 3 or 4 minutes, and cook until *al dente*. Drain and toss with fennel mixture and crumbled feta cheese. Garnish with fennel sprigs.

Serve with a light salad and a Plum Mascarpone Tart with Quick Nut Crust.

♦ Instead of anchovies, use chopped freshly brined sardines or smoked mussels. For a subtler effect, simmer a quarter of the fennel in chicken or fish broth to cover, and purée with a tablespoon of feta in a blender. Thin sauce with more broth or cream and add a dash of Pernod.

◇ The salt from the anchovies and feta, and the licorice flavors from the fennel reach out for fruity, refreshing white wines such as Vouvray Sec and German Kabinett Reisling from the Rhein.

PASTA WITH BLACK BEANS & SUN-DRIED TOMATOES

4 slices pancetta (or bacon)
2 tablespoons olive oil
1 small onion, chopped fine
2 cloves garlic, minced
4 sun-dried tomatoes, diced
1 small fresh red or green chili pepper, seeded
     and minced
¼ cup white wine
1 cup cooked black beans (or fava, pea beans,
     cannellini, Great Northern), plus their
     liquid
Salt and black pepper to taste
⅓ pound dried pasta (macaroni, shells, penne)
Grated Parmesan or Pecorino cheese

Bring 3 quarts of water (with a tablespoon of salt and a teaspoon of oil) to the boil.

Fry pancetta or bacon until crisp, remove, cut in small pieces, and reserve. Pour out all but a teaspoon of fat. Heat the oil with fat and add onion, garlic, tomatoes, and chili pepper. Sauté 4 or 5 minutes until vegetables are softened, add wine, drained beans, and seasoning, and bring to the simmer. (If sauce is too thick, add some of the bean liquid.) Remove from heat and keep sauce warm until ready to use.

Cook pasta in the boiling water, test after 3 or 4 minutes, and cook until *al dente*. Drain and mix the pasta with beans. Serve with grated cheese.

Serve hot with crusty semolina bread and a mixed green or a fresh fruit salad.

♦ Turn pasta and bean combination into a soup, as in pasta e fagioli, by using 3 ounces pasta to 3 cups chicken broth. Mash some of the beans to thicken the liquid and add a couple of seeded and chopped fresh tomatoes.

◊ Sturdy, young red wines, like Nebbiolo d'Alba or Côtes du Rhone Villages are perfect companions to hardy bean pasta dishes.

FETTUCCINE
WITH OYSTERS

1 cup shucked oysters, plus their liquid
3 tablespoons butter
1 teaspoon fresh thyme (or ¼ teaspoon dried
thyme)
Salt and black pepper to taste
¾ cup crème fraîche or heavy cream
1 teaspoon fresh lemon juice
⅓ pound fresh fettuccine
Grated Parmesan cheese
Sprigs of fresh thyme for garnish

Bring 3 quarts of water (with a tablespoon of salt and a teaspoon of oil) to a boil.

Drain oysters and reserve ¼ cup of their liquid. Heat butter in a skillet and sauté oysters gently over medium-low heat, with thyme and seasonings, for 1 or 2 minutes. Add oyster liquid, remove from heat, and stir in the crème fraîche. (If using heavy cream, remove oysters, add oyster liquid and cream to the pan, and reduce until just thickened.) Add lemon juice to taste and keep sauce warm (but not over direct heat) while cooking the pasta.

Cook pasta in boiling water, test after 1 minute, and drain the moment it reaches *al dente*. Immediately toss pasta with sauce and sprinkle with cheese and a few sprigs of fresh thyme.

Serve as a one-dish meal and, for an all-white meal, finish with Pernod Pears.

◆ The same sauce works well with other seafood, such as tiny clams, scallops, crab, or lobster. For a ritzy occasion, garnish the sauce with fresh sturgeon, golden whitefish, or salmon caviar.

◇ Try a Friulian Pinot Bianco, Alsatian Pinot Blanc, or crisp Oregon Chardonnay.

ORZO WITH PINE NUTS
& CURRANTS

3 cups chicken stock
½ cup dried currants
1 cup orzo
1 tablespoon olive oil
4 green onions, chopped
½ cup pine nuts
Salt and black pepper to taste

Bring stock to the boil, add currants and orzo, lower heat, and let liquid simmer for 8 to 10 minutes, or until liquid is largely absorbed and the pasta is *al dente*.

Meanwhile, heat oil in a skillet and sauté onions and pine nuts for 3 or 4 minutes until golden. Add to the orzo, with seasonings, when the pasta is done.

Serve as an accompaniment to a roast lamb, chicken, or rabbit, or to a grilled fish.

♦ Orzo in shape and texture is somewhat like rice. Try mixing it with chopped wild mushrooms, such as chanterelles, dried cherries, or apricots that have been soaked in Madeira.

SWEET LEMON NOODLES
DESSERT PASTA

4 tablespoons butter
½ pound fresh ricotta cheese
½ cup mascarpone
2 to 3 tablespoons sugar
Rind and juice of 1 lemon
⅓ pound fresh fettuccine or other egg noodles

Bring 3 quarts of water (with a tablespoon of salt and a teaspoon of oil) to the boil.

Melt butter in a saucepan. Remove from heat and blend in ricotta and mascarpone until smooth. Add sugar, lemon rind, and juice. Taste and add more sugar if desired.

Cook pasta in boiling water, taste after 1 minute, and drain the moment the pasta is *al dente*. Toss pasta with the sauce.

Serve as a dessert after a light meal, such as Steamed Clams with Vegetables.

♦ For a savory/unsweetened pasta, simply eliminate sugar and make a lemon-flavored cheese sauce. Or, for another form of dessert using ricotta and mascarpone, fill a prebaked pastry crust with the mixture (See Quick Nut Crust, page 196) and sprinkle the top with toasted almonds or candied lemon slices.

◇ Accompany this simple but delicious preparation with an unusual dessert wine, such as a sharp, lemony Malvasia from Sicily.

ORANGE-ALMOND FETTUCCINE
DESSERT PASTA

4 tablespoons butter
Rind and juice of 2 oranges
1/3 cup sugar
1/2 teaspoon ground cinnamon
1/4 teaspoon black pepper
1/3 pound fresh fettuccine
1/2 cup toasted almonds, chopped
1/3 cup grated Parmesan cheese

Bring 3 quarts of water (with a tablespoon of salt and a teaspoon of oil) to a boil.

Melt butter in a saucepan. Reserve orange rind but add just ¾ cup of orange juice to butter. Add sugar and turn heat to high until liquid begins to turn amber. Remove from heat, add rind, cinnamon, and pepper.

Cook pasta in the boiling water, test after 1 minute, and drain the moment the pasta is *al dente*. Toss with sauce and sprinkle it with nuts and cheese.

Serve after a meal of Turkey Scallopini and Onion-Berry Confit.

◆ For a molded and baked pasta dessert, use but ¼ cup orange juice beaten with 2 eggs and ½ pound fresh ricotta or farmer's cheese. Add the other ingredients as above. Sprinkle a buttered 1-quart mold with Parmesan cheese and alternate layers of cooked fettuccine with cheese mixture. Bake at 375°F. for 20 to 30 minutes until top is browned. Unmold and serve.

◇ For an interesting twist, serve this dessert with a sweet white, such as nutty Tuscan Vin Santo.

PASTA WITH
ARTICHOKES & OLIVES

2 large artichokes
1 tablespoon olive oil
Juice of ½ lemon
1 tablespoon butter
½ small onion, chopped
½ cup green olives, Mediterranean style
½ cup heavy cream
Salt and black pepper to taste
⅓ pound fresh tagliatelle
Grated Parmesan cheese

Leave the full stems on artichokes but tear off all the fibrous outer leaves and trim off the base of the leaves all around to get to the outside of the heart. Cut off and discard the top half of the artichokes. Cut the bottom half into quarters or eighths and carve out the chokes (small hairs on top of the heart). Simmer artichokes in ⅔ cup water with oil and lemon juice, in a covered pan, for about 10 minutes, or until artichokes are tender.

Remove artichokes, add butter and onion, and simmer 4 or 5 minutes, or until onions are softened. Pit the green olives and add olives and artichokes to the onions. Add cream, season, and bring to the simmer. Keep sauce warm until ready to use.

Bring 3 quarts of water (with a tablespoon of salt and a teaspoon of oil) to the boil. Add pasta, test after 1 minute, and drain the moment it reaches *al dente*. Toss with the sauce and serve with Parmesan cheese and an extra sprinkling of black pepper.

Serve as a main dish after Wok-Smoked Trout or Roasted Oysters with Curry Butter.

♦   If you don't have time to prepare fresh artichokes, buy artichoke hearts preserved in oil or cook frozen artichoke hearts and then sauté them in oil with the onion. Increase flavor with fresh herbs, such as mint, oregano, or chopped parsley.

◇   Artichokes can pose problems for some wines—turning them dull and insipid—but crisp, fruity Italian wines, like Sauvignon Blancs and Pinot Grigios from Friuli, do just fine.

SHELLFISH

STEAMED CLAMS WITH VEGETABLES
♦ SALSA SQUID ♦ CHARRED
SHRIMP POBLANO ♦ WOK-SMOKED
SCALLOPS WITH GREEN SAUCE ♦
CLAM & SAUSAGE CHOWDER ♦
HOT POTATO SALAD WITH MUSSELS
♦ SCALLOPS WITH HAZELNUTS ♦
LOBSTER WITH AVOCADO & TEQUILA

STEAMED CLAMS
WITH VEGETABLES

1 dozen hard-shell clams (littleneck, cherry-
 stone, or Manila)
1 small turnip
1 small onion
1 large carrot
1 clove garlic
¼ cup fresh parsley
¼ cup fresh cilantro
4 tablespoons butter
Black pepper to taste
⅓ cup white wine

Scrub clams thoroughly and rinse under cold running water.

Dice turnip, onion, and carrot. Mince garlic, parsley, and cilantro.

Melt butter in a wide-bottomed pan with a close-fitting lid. Sauté vegetables and herbs over low heat for about 5 minutes, until slightly softened. Season with pepper, add wine and clams, and cover pan tightly. Steam until clams open, about 7 to 10 minutes.

Remove clams to a bowl until their shells are cool enough to handle. Discard shells and add clams and their broth to vegetable mixture. Serve in soup bowls with additional fresh cilantro if desired.

Serve with Pesto Spaghetti Squash and finish with a good ripe cheese.

♦   Mussels are delicious prepared in the same way and, for a variant in seasoning, add a few strands of saffron to the vegetables when sautéing them.

◊   Crisp, fruity young Loire white wines, like Muscadet, Sancerre, and Pouilly Fumé, are ideal for steamed clams.

SALSA SQUID

1 pound squid, cleaned
4 tablespoons olive oil
2 tablespoons fresh lime juice
2 teaspoons red or white wine vinegar
1 small red onion, chopped
1 sweet red pepper, chopped
1 tomato, seeded and chopped
1 jalapeño pepper, seeded and minced
¼ cup chopped fresh cilantro
Salt and black pepper to taste

Cut the body of the squid crosswise into rings, leaving the tentacles whole. Heat oil in a large skillet over moderate heat and sauté squid gently for 1 or 2 minutes, just long enough to turn flesh opaque (be careful not to overcook). Add remaining ingredients to squid, adding salt and pepper to taste, and serve at room temperature.

Half the quantity makes a good starter and, like a seviche, tastes great with margaritas. If you serve it as an entree, accompany it with a soothing carbohydrate like Green Rice or Red Lentils.

♦   The same salsa will accommodate a wide variety of additions, such as shrimp and scallops, cubes of grilled tuna, cubes of avocado, quartered hard-cooked eggs, and fresh corn kernels.

◊   Inexpensive sparkling wines from Spain, Australia, and California are every bit as good as beer at extinguishing jalapeño-induced bonfires.

CHARRED SHRIMP POBLANO

1 pound medium or large shrimp in their shells
1 cup white wine (or water)
2 tomatoes
2 whole cloves garlic, peeled
1 chili poblano (see Note) or 2 jalapeños
1 small onion, cut in eighths
2 tablespoons olive oil
3 tablespoons chopped fresh cilantro
Salt to taste

Peel and devein shrimp and put shells in a small saucepan with water or white wine. Bring liquid to the boil, cover, and cook 15 minutes. Remove shells and boil liquid down to ¼ cup.

Put tomatoes, garlic, chili, and onion in a small oiled baking pan and dribble over them 1 tablespoon of olive oil. Roast uncovered at 400°F. for about 30 minutes, until onion is soft. When the chili is cool enough to handle, remove and discard the stem, cut chili in half and remove seeds. Process chili, tomatoes, garlic, and onion in a blender. Add cilantro, salt, and reserved shrimp liquid, and purée until smooth.

Heat a wok or large cast-iron skillet over high heat. Put in remaining tablespoon of oil and when it begins to smoke, add shrimp, turning to char on all sides. Put sauce on a platter and place shrimp on top.

Serve as a first course for Fresh Corn Tamale Pie or as a main dish with Roast Potato Chips or Honeyed Golden Peppers.

♦ If you want to char the shrimp in their shells (as in Chinese Shrimp-in-the-Shell), serve the sauce as a dipping sauce. Or serve with the fresh salsa used in Salsa Squid.

◇ Crisp, fresh Fino sherry, served ice-cold, is a terrific accompaniment to this tapas-like preparation.

NOTE: If you use a dried poblano (called chili ancho), rinse it, remove stem and seeds, then toast for a minute or two in a hot skillet, and add to the shrimp shells and wine. Instead of discarding it with the shells, put chili in the blender to purée with the other blender ingredients.

WOK-SMOKED SCALLOPS
WITH GREEN SAUCE

1 pound sea scallops
¼ cup black tea
¼ cup brown rice
¼ cup brown sugar

SAUCE
¼ cup fresh parsley
¼ cup fresh cilantro
2 cloves garlic, mashed
1 tablespoon white wine vinegar
1 tablespoon sour cream
2 tablespoons lime juice
1 teaspoon salt
¼ teaspoon freshly ground cumin
Pinch of cayenne pepper

Cut large scallops in half to make 2 thin rounds. Line a wok with foil and put the smoking mixture—tea, rice, and sugar—in middle of the foil. Cover tightly with a foil-lined lid and place wok over high heat for 5 minutes. Place scallops in a single layer on a mesh rack or on a rack covered with foil (slit foil in several places so the smoke will come through). Place rack in wok, cover with lid, and smoke over high heat for 5 minutes. Remove from heat and let sit, covered, for 10 minutes.

Prepare sauce by puréeing the ingredients in a blender. Pour sauce on a platter and heap scallops on top of the sauce.

Serve with Apricot Sweet Potatoes or with Wok-Grilled Fennel, cooked in the wok before you cook the scallops.

♦ Almost any kind of shellfish or fish does well with this sort of smoking and this kind of sauce. For an herb flavor without the bother of smoking, sauté the scallops in a little butter and oil and serve with the same sauce.

◇ Smoky Kabinett Rieslings, especially from Rheingau, are great for pan-smoked shellfish.

CLAM & SAUSAGE CHOWDER

1 dozen hard-shelled clams (littleneck, cherry-
    stone, or Manila)
1 cup dry white wine
¼ pound hot Italian sausage
1 potato, cubed
½ head fennel, sliced crosswise
1 green or red bell pepper, sliced crosswise
1 small onion, sliced in rings
2 cloves garlic, minced
2 large tomatoes, seeded and chopped
2 sprigs fresh oregano (or ½ teaspoon dried
    oregano)
Black and cayenne peppers to taste
⅓ cup chopped fresh Italian parsley

Scrub clams thoroughly and rinse under cold running water. Put with wine in a saucepan with a tight lid. Steam over medium heat for about 6 to 8 minutes, or until barely open. Remove from heat and set aside.

Slice sausage in chunks and sauté in a large skillet until some fat is released. Add potato and brown with sausage. Add fennel, bell pepper, onion, and garlic, and brown lightly. Add tomatoes, oregano, and peppers.

Strain clam liquor through doubled cheesecloth or a kitchen towel and add the liquor to the vegetables. Cover skillet and simmer gently for 10 minutes, or until potatoes are fork-tender. Add clams in their shells for the last 3 minutes to warm them. Sprinkle with parsley and serve from skillet.

Serve with crusty bread and Sweet Lemon Noodles for dessert.

◆ Clams are also wonderful with cubed pork, as the Portuguese know. Substitute ½ pound boneless pork, cubed, for the sausage and proceed as above.

◇ Try a full-bodied rosé from Tavel, or a light red wine from Provence.

HOT POTATO SALAD
WITH MUSSELS

1 quart mussels
½ cup dry white wine
1 clove garlic, minced
¼ cup minced fresh parsley
1 leek
4 new potatoes, skins on
⅓ cup olive oil
2 tablespoons balsamic vinegar
Salt and black pepper to taste
Chives for garnish

Scrub mussels thoroughly, rinse under cold running water, and pull off beards. Put in a tight-lidded pan with wine, garlic, and parsley. Steam over medium heat for 3 to 5 minutes, or until shells open. Remove pan from heat and set aside.

Cut leek in half just down to the root end, rinse thoroughly to remove sand from inner layers. Cut off root end and most of green top. Slice crosswise.

Pour mussel liquor into a saucepan, bring it to the boil. Add leek and new potatoes and boil, covered, about 10 minutes, or until tender. Remove and cool enough to slice potatoes. Place them with the drained leek on a platter.

Remove mussels from their shells, add to leek and sliced potatoes, and dress with a vinaigrette made of the oil, vinegar, and seasonings. Sprinkle with chopped chives.

Serve with Red Pepper–Garlic Soup and follow with Banana Zabaglione.

♦   Turn this into a kind of salade Niçoise by adding parboiled green beans, black and green olives, hard-cooked eggs, and chunks of grilled tuna.

◇   Crisp, light white wines like Verdicchio and Village Chablis are fine accompaniments to steamed mussels.

SCALLOPS WITH HAZELNUTS

½ cup hazelnuts, skins on
4 tablespoons butter
1 pound sea scallops
¼ teaspoon ground cumin
⅛ teaspoon ground nutmeg
Salt and black pepper to taste
Lime juice to taste

Chop nuts to medium-fine in a food processor. Heat butter in a large skillet until it begins to brown. Toast nuts in the butter for 1 to 2 minutes.

If scallops are large, slice them in half to make 2 thin rounds. Add scallops, cumin, nutmeg, and seasonings to skillet. Sauté scallops gently for about 2 minutes, or just until they turn opaque (do not overcook). Squeeze a little lime juice over the scallops and serve.

Good with a crisp salad like the Brie-Arugula Salad with Balsamic Cream Dressing or, for color contrast, Hot Beet Salad.

♦   If you like to use scallop shells, mix scallops with a light cream sauce thickened with onion instead of flour. Sauté a small chopped onion in 2 tablespoons butter, add ⅔ cup heavy cream with seasonings, and purée in a blender. Add the scallops to the sauce, place them in a single layer in 4 shells arranged on a cookie sheet or baking pan. Cover with ¼ cup chopped nuts mixed with the same amount of fresh bread crumbs, browned in 3 or 4 tablespoons butter. Bake at 375°F. for 10 to 12 minutes (depending on size), or until the scallops are opaque. Squeeze lime over the tops before serving.

◇   Scallops' sweetness pairs beautifully with white wines that have a trace of sweetness themselves. Look for Vouvray Sec or Dry California Chenin Blanc.

LOBSTER WITH
AVOCADO & TEQUILA

1 large lobster (2 to 3 pounds)
4 tablespoons butter
Salt and black pepper to taste
3 green onions with tops, chopped
¼ cup fish stock or white wine
¼ cup tequila
½ ripe avocado
Rind and juice of 1 lime

Hold live lobster firmly on a cutting board and dispatch it (quickly and humanely) by inserting a strong knife in the slot between the tail and the body and pushing the blade down until it touches the board. Cut up lobster over a wide bowl in order to save all juices. Slit open the underside of the tail with a pair of kitchen scissors and extract the meat. Cut through the underside of the body with scissors and extract any green tomalley (liver) or red coral (roe). Crack claws and legs and extract meat. Cut tail meat in chunks about the size of the claw meat.

Melt butter in medium sauté pan. Season lobster pieces with salt and pepper and sauté with the green onions for 2 minutes. Add lobster juices, fish stock, and tequila, and simmer for 3 or 4 minutes, or until lobster just turns opaque. Remove lobster and pour its liquid and onions into a blender. Add avocado in chunks, plus the lime juice, and purée. Thin sauce if necessary with more tequila. Pour sauce onto a platter, put the lobster on top, and sprinkle it with grated lime rind.

Serve this rich dish with a light salad like Thai Papaya and end with Jalapeño-Lime Ice.

♦   Lobster and cubes of avocado make a good salad, just as crab and avocado do. Steam the lobster ahead, cut up the meat, combine it with avocado, and minced red onion, and dress it with a lime vinaigrette flavored with fresh cilantro.

◇ Light- to medium-bodied Sauvignon Blancs and Chardonnays from California—provided they aren't too alcoholic—are fine partners for this Southwestern plate.

FISH

RARE TUNA WITH TAPENADE ♦
WALNUT-CRUSTED FLOUNDER
♦ MAKO SHARK PROVENÇAL ♦
BLUEFISH IN BALSAMIC
♦ PEPPER SALMON STEAKS ♦
ROASTED GARLIC COD ♦ FISH
CHOWDER WITH CHICK-PEAS ♦
COCONUT SNAPPER

RARE TUNA
WITH TAPENADE

1 pound tuna (two 1-inch-thick steaks)

TAPENADE
¼ cup olive oil
½ cup green olives, Mediterranean style
1 clove garlic, mashed
2 teaspoons mashed anchovies (or anchovy
   paste)
1 teaspoon Dijon mustard
1 tablespoon lemon juice
1 tablespoon chopped fresh Italian parsley

Brush tuna on both sides with a little of the oil. Heat a wok or heavy skillet over high heat until smoking. Sear tuna on both sides, about 3 to 5 minutes per side. Remove fish and cut it in thin slices.

Make tapenade by puréeing the remaining ingredients in a blender. If mixture is too thick, add more oil (or a little white wine) to thin it.

Mound the tapenade in the middle of a platter and surround it with slices of tuna.

Serve with Kale & Red Pepper Sauté or Red Lentils.

♦ For an unusual flavor, use a miso paste with toasted Nori seaweed (available in health food stores). In a blender, purée 2 tablespoons miso and 1 toasted Nori sheet with 2 tablespoons oil, 1 tablespoon vinegar, 1 teaspoon soy sauce, 1 teaspoon chopped ginger, and ¼ teaspoon toasted and ground Szechuan peppercorns.

◊ Sharp, fruity red wines, like Chinon and Bourgueil, go beautifully with rare tuna.

WALNUT-CRUSTED FLOUNDER

1 pound flounder fillets
Salt and black and cayenne peppers to taste
½ cup walnuts, ground
1 tablespoon each of butter and olive oil

Season fillets on both sides with salt and peppers. Press walnuts into fillets on both sides, as if breading them. Heat butter and oil in a skillet over moderate heat, add fillets, and brown for 4 minutes on one side. Turn and brown the other side 1 or 2 minutes only, or until fish has just turned opaque.

Because there is no sauce, you might serve this with a pasta such as Pasta with Artichokes & Olives or Penne with Charred Vegetables.

♦   Almonds or pecans can also be used as a coating for the fish. For an unusual variant, try ground sunflower or pumpkin seeds. Be careful to keep the heat low enough so as not to burn nuts or seeds.

◇   Barrel-fermented Chardonnays from California and Australia, with their pronounced toastiness, complement the nutty flavors in this simple but tasty fish dish.

MAKO SHARK
PROVENÇAL

6 cloves garlic
1 sweet red pepper
2 shallots
2 tablespoons olive oil
2 sprigs fresh rosemary (or ½ teaspoon dried
     rosemary)
1 pound mako shark steaks
Salt and black pepper to taste
1 tomato, seeded and chopped
½ cup fish stock
1 cup dry red wine
Fresh rosemary sprigs for garnish

Peel garlic, halve and seed red pepper, and peel shallots. Put olive oil in a baking pan large enough to hold the fish, put vegetables in the pan and roll them in the oil, add rosemary, and roast at 400°F. for 15 to 20 minutes. Remove pan and lower heat to 350°F.

Brush fish with the olive oil in the pan. Heat a wok or cast-iron skillet until smoking and sear the fish quickly on both sides. Season with salt and pepper and put in baking pan with roasted vegetables. Add tomato, stock, and wine, and bake at 350°F. for 8 to 10 minutes, or until fish is fork-tender.

Remove steaks to a serving dish until they are cool enough to trim out the bone and remove skin. Slice crosswise and surround with roasted vegetables. Garnish with sprigs of rosemary and serve in soup bowls.

Finish the meal with Jalapeño-Lime Ice or a bowl of fresh fruit.

♦   Since shark is a fish that can take strong flavors, try braising it with lemons and onions. Sear it first or not, as you choose, then add it to a baking pan in which a thinly sliced lemon and red onion have cooked in the red wine.

◇   Look for light, fruity red wines from Provence and Northern Italy, such as Bandol and Dolcetta d'Alba.

BLUEFISH
IN BALSAMIC

1 pound bluefish fillets
1 tablespoon olive oil
Salt and black pepper to taste
2 green onions, chopped
¼ cup red or white wine
1 tablespoon balsamic vinegar
6 or 7 fresh basil leaves

Roll fillets in the oil in a nonmetal baking dish and season with salt and pepper on both sides. Sprinkle with the onions, add wine, vinegar, and half the basil. Cover dish tightly with foil and bake at 350°F. for 8 to 10 minutes, depending on thickness of the fillets. Garnish with remaining basil.

Serve with Thai Papaya Salad or Red Lentils.

♦ Because of its oil, bluefish does well grilled or broiled. If you have time and like Chinese flavors, before grilling, marinate fish for half an hour in ¼ cup soy sauce, 1 tablespoon sesame oil, 1 or 2 slices fresh gingerroot (chopped), and ½ teaspoon Japanese wasabi mustard.

◇ Try light, acidic white wines with little or no trace of wood, such as New York Chardonnay and Alto Pinot Grigio.

PEPPER
SALMON STEAKS

2 tablespoons black peppercorns
1 teaspoon Szechuan peppercorns
1 pound salmon steaks or fillets
Salt to taste
1 tablespoon sesame oil
¼ cup dry sherry

Crush or grind both kinds of peppercorns coarsely and press into salmon on both sides. Salt lightly. Heat a wok or heavy cast-iron skillet over high heat until smoking. Add oil and then salmon. Sear salmon on both sides, lower heat, then add sherry carefully because it will flame. Cooking time depends on thickness of steak or fillet. If salmon is less than an inch thick, cook it less than 2 to 3 minutes a side.

Serve with Appled Eggplant, Turnip-Pear Purée, or Tahini Broccoli.

♦   Different spices, used the same way, will produce different but also delicious effects. Coarsely grind a mixture of cumin and coriander, or fennel seeds. Or, try a dusting of allspice or Chinese 5-spice powder.

◇   Spicy salmon loves a refreshing, young rosé, like a Rosé d'Anjou or Vin Gris de Pinot Noir, to cool its flames.

ROASTED
GARLIC COD

15 cloves garlic, unpeeled
½ cup olive oil
½ teaspoon Dijon mustard
2 teaspoons lemon juice or vinegar
Salt and black pepper to taste
1 pound cod steaks or fillets
½ cup white wine
Sprigs of fresh parsley for garnish

Brush garlic with a little of the oil and roast it in foil at 375°F. for 20 minutes. Squeeze garlic flesh from skins and blend with oil, mustard, lemon, and seasonings until smooth, making a thick mayonnaise.

Poach cod in the wine in a covered skillet over moderate heat for 6 to 10 minutes, or until cod is just fork-tender. Remove cod to a serving platter. Thin garlic sauce in blender by adding ¼ cup of poaching liquid. Pour sauce over the cod. Garnish with fresh parsley.

Serve with boiled new potatoes and a light salad, followed by good cheese and fruit.

◆ Another complement to cod is leeks. Clean 4 leeks well, cut in half crosswise, then lengthwise, and slice in thin strips (julienne). Stew in a skillet in 6 tablespoons butter for 6 to 8 minutes to soften. Remove half the leeks, add cod, cover with remaining leeks, season, cover skillet with a lid, and steam cod for 6 to 10 minutes.

◇ Serve with a crisp, light white wine like a Trebbiano or Alsatian Sylvaner.

FISH CHOWDER
WITH CHICK-PEAS

½ head fennel, sliced, with green tops
1 sweet red pepper, seeded and chopped
1 small red chili pepper, seeded and diced
1 small onion, chopped
1 clove garlic, minced
Pinch of saffron
2 to 3 slices gingerroot, minced
2 tablespoons olive oil
1 pound monkfish (or similar sturdy fish)
Salt and black pepper to taste
1½ cups cooked chick-peas
2 cups fish stock or clam juice
1 cup plain yogurt

Put fennel, sweet and red chili peppers, onion, garlic, saffron, and ginger in a large saucepan with the olive oil. Sauté the vegetables gently for 2 to 3 minutes, to slightly soften.

Cut monkfish into 2-inch cubes and add to saucepan. Season lightly.

Put half the chick-peas in a blender with half the stock and purée until smooth. Add the purée with remaining stock, chick-peas, and yogurt to saucepan. Bring liquid to the simmer and cook fish 3 or 4 minutes over low heat, or until just fork-tender.

Serve with an Indian bread like nan or chapati and end the meal with Grape Freezies or Gingered Figs.

♦   Monkfish is also good with lentils. Substitute 1½ cups cooked yellow lentils for the chick-peas and proceed as above.

◇   Try this Indian-inspired seafood soup with a medium-bodied German Riesling, such as a Spätlese Halbtrocken or Trocken from the Rheinhessen.

COCONUT SNAPPER

2 tablespoons olive oil
1 small onion, chopped
1 clove garlic, minced
1 jalapeño pepper, seeded and minced
2 or 3 slices gingerroot, minced
¼ cup canned sweetened coconut cream
½ cup fish stock or clam juice
Salt and pepper to taste
1 pound red snapper fillets
2 tablespoons fresh lime juice

Heat oil and sauté onion, garlic, jalapeño, and ginger gently until softened. Stir in coconut cream and fish stock. Season snapper fillets and add to the mixture in the pan. Spoon some of the sauce over the fish. Cover pan and poach fish gently over low heat 4 to 7 minutes, or until just fork-tender. Squeeze lime over the fish and remove fish to a serving platter. Pour sauce over the fish.

Serve with Thai Papaya Salad and lemon squares for dessert.

◆ Since snapper is a beautiful fish to serve whole, try steaming it, Oriental style, in a wok with ½ cup water in the bottom. Make 3 deep parallel cuts on each side of the fish. Place the fish on a dish that will fit into the wok, with flavorings on top, and cover tightly. Use the same flavorings as above, substituting green onions for onion and diluting the coconut cream with lime juice, omitting the stock. Cover with a tight lid and steam 15 to 20 minutes for a 1½ to 2 pound fish, 20 to 25 for a 3-pounder.

◇ Gewürztraminers, which often suggest coconut and other tropical fruits, pair well with exotic, slightly sweet preparations. Look for examples from Northern Italy and the cooler parts of California.

BIRDS

PUMPKIN-SEED QUAIL ◆ COCONUT
CHICKEN WITH LEMON GRASS ◆
DUCK BREASTS WITH BLACK BEAN
SAUCE ◆ CHICKEN GUACAMOLE
TORTILLAS ◆ TURKEY
SCALLOPPINI ◆ BARBADOS
CHICKEN ◆ SQUAB & RABE

PUMPKIN-SEED
QUAIL

4 quail
Salt and black pepper to taste
Flour and cornmeal, mixed
2 tablespoons each of olive oil and butter
½ cup shelled pumpkin seeds
2 jalapeño peppers, charred (see Note)
1 clove garlic
¼ onion, chopped
¼ teaspoon ground cumin
1⅓ cups chicken stock
2 sprigs cilantro for garnish

Split each quail along the back, spread it open, and flatten. Clip off the backbone with a pair of kitchen shears. Season birds on both sides with salt and pepper and dust with a mixture of flour and cornmeal.

Heat oil and butter in a heavy skillet, sear quail on both sides, lower heat and sauté 3 to 4 minutes, until tender. Remove and keep warm.

In same skillet, toast pumpkin seeds 3 or 4 minutes (cover the skillet partially because the seeds will pop up; stir them once or twice to prevent burning). Remove seeds to a blender with the jalapeños. Brown garlic and onion in same pan, add cumin and chicken stock and scrape mixture into blender. Add any juices from reserved quail. Purée and pour sauce onto a platter, lay quail on top, and garnish with cilantro.

Serve with Appled Eggplant and finish with Chocolate-Chili Cream.

♦ Quail take well to wok-smoking (see Wok-Smoked Trout). Season and smoke whole quail for the same time as the trout.

◇ Oregon Pinot Noir or red Burgundy from the Côte de Beaune are great with small birds.

NOTE: Char peppers by holding them with a pair of tongs over a direct flame until their skins blacken on all sides. Remove stems and seeds, but for this sauce leave the skins on.

COCONUT CHICKEN
WITH LEMON GRASS

1 tablespoon vegetable oil
Salt and black pepper to taste
1½ pounds chicken thighs and legs
4 green onions, chopped
2 cloves garlic, minced
1 small fresh red or green chili pepper, seeded
  and minced
1 teaspoon ground coriander
½ teaspoon turmeric
½ teaspoon powdered lemon grass (or 1 fresh
  blade) (see Note)
1 tomato or sweet red pepper, seeded and
  chopped
¼ cup canned sweetened coconut cream
¾ cup chicken stock
2 tablespoons fresh lime juice, or to taste

Heat oil in a large skillet, season chicken, and brown it on all sides. Add onions, garlic, chili, coriander, and turmeric and sauté for 3 or 4 minutes, until softened.

Add remaining ingredients, except for lime juice, lower heat, and cover pan. Simmer gently for 20 to 25 minutes, or until chicken is fork-tender. Remove from heat, taste sauce, and add lime juice accordingly.

Serve with plain rice or a mix of rice and lentils.

♦   An easy way to cook a whole chicken is to use the same flavorings as above, but instead of sautéing chicken pieces, brown chicken as above, then braise in a covered earthenware pot, like a Schlemmertopf; or, wrap tightly in banana leaves in foil.

◇   Try with sparkling Rieslings from Germany (called Sekt) or Alsace (called Crémant d'Alsace).

NOTE: Dried lemon grass is available at most health food stores in the form of lemon grass tea.

DUCK BREASTS
WITH BLACK BEAN SAUCE

2 whole duck breasts (4 pieces)
Black pepper to taste
2 tablespoons peanut oil

SAUCE
1 tablespoon peanut oil
2 cloves garlic, minced
4 to 5 slices gingerroot, minced
2 tablespoons fermented black beans, chopped
⅓ cup dry sherry
1 teaspoon sugar
½ teaspoon soy sauce

Season breasts with pepper and sear in 2 tablespoons oil in a heavy skillet, browning about 2 minutes a side to keep them rare within. Remove duck to a platter and cut each breast into thin slices.

Heat 1 tablespoon peanut oil in same skillet; sauté garlic, ginger, and beans 1 to 2 minutes. Add sherry, sugar, and soy sauce, scrape in any pan juices, and pour sauce over the duck.

Good with Chinese Greens with Pesto or Tahini Broccoli.

♦ Duck takes as well to Southwest flavors as to Chinese, so try the same duck method with a Poblano Sauce, using ¼ cup chicken stock as a base (see Charred Shrimp Poblano).

◇ The slight sweetness in this dish makes a fruity red wine such as Beaujolais or California Gamay feel right at home.

CHICKEN GUACAMOLE TORTILLAS

1 pair chicken breasts (about 1 pound), boned
    and skinned
Salt and black and cayenne peppers to taste
½ teaspoon ground cumin
1 tablespoon olive oil

GUACAMOLE
1 ripe avocado
1 jalapeño or serrano pepper, seeded and
    minced
½ small red onion, chopped
1 clove garlic, minced
1 small tomato, seeded and diced
2 tablespoons chopped fresh cilantro
Salt and black and cayenne peppers to taste
Fresh lime juice to taste

2 large flour tortillas
½ cup sour cream

Season chicken breasts on both sides with salt, peppers, and cumin, and sauté in hot oil 3 to 4 minutes a side, until golden. Remove and slice thin.

Make guacamole by mashing avocado, adding other ingredients, and seasoning to taste with salt, peppers, and lime juice.

Lay half the chicken slices in one of the tortillas, cover with half the guacamole, and roll up tortilla. Repeat. Serve with sour cream on the side for dipping.

For a big meal, serve with Fresh Corn Tamale Pie and end with Jalapeño-Lime Ice.

◆ For another version, lay chicken slices on flat tortillas, cover with Poblano Sauce (see Charred Shrimp Poblano), topped with grated Monterey Jack cheese, and serve open-faced without rolling the tortillas.

◇ Try California Sauvignon Blancs that have been blended with some Sémillon for added richness.

TURKEY SCALLOPINI

1 fresh turkey breast (about ¾ pound)
Salt and black pepper to taste
¼ cup heavy cream
⅓ cup fresh bread crumbs
⅓ cup grated Parmesan cheese
1 tablespoon each of *olive oil and butter*
¼ cup Madeira (Marsala, Port, or sherry)

Slice breast crosswise and pound each slice thin with a mallet or thick plate edge. Season well, dip each slice into cream, bread crumbs, and then cheese to coat both sides.

Heat oil and butter in a large skillet and brown turkey over moderate heat, about 1 minute a side (for ¼-inch slices), or until just cooked through. Don't overcook. Remove to a platter. Add Madeira and cook over high heat for 1 minute, stirring in all pan juices. Pour sauce over turkey.

Serve with Onion-Berry Confit or Turnip-Pear Purée.

♦ Prepackaged turkey breast is undervalued because it is convenient and cheap, but for those very reasons it's good to use in a variety of ways. One way is to braise it whole, in a small covered casserole, with soy, ginger, chili oil, and Chinese vegetables such as straw mushrooms, fresh water chestnuts, and strips of sweet red pepper.

◇ Try a QbA Riesling from the Mosel, or a light Riesling from Washington State.

BARBADOS CHICKEN

4 chicken pieces, for frying
Salt and black pepper to taste
Flour
2 tablespoons butter
2 oranges
2 teaspoons Dijon mustard
2 or 3 dashes of Tabasco sauce
2 tablespoons orange marmalade
2 tablespoons dark rum

Season chicken well on all sides and roll in the flour. Heat butter in a skillet and sauté the chicken until evenly browned, about 6 or 10 minutes.

Grate rind of 1 orange and squeeze its juice into a cup. Mix in mustard, Tabasco, marmalade, and rum and adjust this particular mixture of sweet and hot to your taste. (Add lemon if too sweet.) Add sauce to chicken, cover skillet, and simmer 10 to 25 minutes (depending on size), until chicken is tender. Use second orange, peeled and segmented, for garnish.

Serve with Chinese Greens with Pesto or Brie-Arugula Salad with Balsamic Cream Dressing.

♦   Enlarge the Barbados reference by frying the chicken with a peeled and sliced plantain, or with a firm sliced banana, browned in a separate pan and used as garnish.

◇   This sweet, spicy dish calls for a tall, cool bottle of Kabinett Riesling from the Rhein, or a thirst-quenching white Zinfandel.

SQUAB & RABE

1 tablespoon olive oil
2 squabs (or pigeons), about 1 pound each
Salt and black pepper to taste
4 green onions, chopped fine
1 clove garlic, minced
½ pound broccoli rabe, chopped
2 tablespoons butter
½ cup chicken stock
¼ cup dry vermouth
2 tablespoons Campari

Heat olive oil in a large skillet and brown squabs on both sides, 2 to 3 minutes per side. Season well and add onions, garlic, and broccoli rabe. Brown 2 or 3 minutes more, then lower heat, add butter, chicken stock, vermouth, and Campari, and simmer birds in sauce 15 to 20 minutes, until tender but still rare. Serve hot or at room temperature.

For contrast to the bitterness of the rabe and Campari, accompany the birds with Apricot Sweet Potatoes or Onion-Berry Confit.

♦   If squabs are hard to come by, substitute a pair of quail for each squab. Season and sauté over high heat, then lower heat and sauté until tender, 3 to 4 minutes for split quail, double the time for whole. Remove to a platter and proceed with the other ingredients.

◇   The light bitterness of the rabe and Campari in this preparation might thin out lighter red wines: better to pair it with a medium-bodied Australian or California Cabernet.

MEATS

PICADILLO ◆ PORK IN PLUM
SAUCE ◆ DILLED YOGURT LAMB
◆ TUSCAN LIVER SAUTÉ ◆
HONEY-MUSTARD SPARERIBS ◆
LAMB WITH APRICOTS & ALMONDS
◆ VENISON WITH MUSTARD FRUITS
◆ BEEF & WILD MUSHROOM
SAUTÉ ◆ VEAL CHOPS WITH
PANCETTA & GOAT CHEESE ◆
STAR-ANISE BEEF WITH SNOW PEAS

PICADILLO

¼ cup currants
2 tablespoons olive oil
1 small onion, chopped fine
1 fresh red or green chili pepper, seeded and
    minced
2 cloves garlic, minced
½ pound each of ground beef and ground pork
½ cup stuffed green olives, sliced
½ green apple, diced
2 tablespoons tomato purée
1 tablespoon cider vinegar
1 tablespoon capers, drained
1 teaspoon salt
½ teaspoon each of ground cumin and oregano
¼ teaspoon each of ground cinnamon and
    cloves

Soak currants in hot water to cover for 15 minutes.

Heat oil in a large skillet and sauté onion, pepper, and garlic for 2 to 3 minutes, or until softened. Increase heat, add beef and pork, and lightly brown meats.

Add remaining ingredients, plus currants and their liquid. Cover and simmer for 10 minutes, then remove lid and cook another 5 to 10 minutes to evaporate some of the liquid.

Serve with Apricot Sweet Potatoes or Pesto Spaghetti Squash.

♦   Make a small molded meat loaf from the same ingredients. Mix sautéed onion, chili pepper, and garlic with raw meats and remaining ingredients, and mix well. Put mixture into a small baking dish and bake at 375°F. for 25 to 30 minutes, or until top is browned.

◇   This happy jumble of sweet and spicy flavors is a fine partner to light, fruity red wines like Beaujolais and Côtes-du-Rhône.

PORK IN
PLUM SAUCE

1 pound pork tenderloin
Salt and black pepper to taste
1 tablespoon olive oil
4 red-skinned plums, such as Santa Clara
1 cup hearty red wine, such as burgundy
½ teaspoon ground cardamom
¼ teaspoon ground cinnamon
⅛ teaspoon ground cloves

Heat a heavy skillet; season pork and brown it well on all sides in oil, for about 10 minutes (or roast at 450°F. for 10 to 15 minutes). Remove to a warm platter.

Halve plums, remove pits, and quarter each half. Add plums, wine, and seasonings to skillet, cover, and simmer over low heat for 10 to 15 minutes, or until tender.

Slice pork crosswise and garnish with half the plums. Put remaining plums in a blender with the liquid and purée. Pour sauce over pork and plums.

Excellent with Apricot Sweet Potatoes or Honeyed Golden Peppers.

◆ Make a similar sauce with prunes and brandy. Soak ½ cup prunes in boiling water. Simmer the prunes in their liquid with the seasonings, and add ¼ cup brandy for the final 3 or 4 minutes.

◇ This dish practically begs for a young, fruity Pinot Noir from Oregon or from a cooler part of California.

DILLED
YOGURT LAMB

2 large loin lamb chops (about 1½ pounds), cut
      thick
Salt and black pepper to taste
2 tablespoons olive oil
1 red onion, sliced
4 cloves garlic, chopped
1 cup plain yogurt
2 tablespoons crumbled feta cheese
3 tablespoons chopped fresh dill
1 tablespoon chopped fresh cilantro

Season lamb and sear it on all sides in the oil. Remove chops and set aside.

In the same pan, sauté onion and garlic 3 to 4 minutes, or until softened. Remove pan from the heat and stir in yogurt, cheese, and half the fresh herbs.

Return chops to pan, cover, and simmer over very low heat about 10 to 15 minutes, or until meat is tender. Remove chops to platter, pour sauce over them, and garnish with remaining herbs.

Serve with Green Rice.

◆ A dilled yogurt sauce is also fine for a lamb loin, pan-grilled or broiled to keep it rare. Purée the sautéed onion and garlic with ½ cup yogurt, 4 tablespoons feta cheese, and ½ tablespoon balsamic vinegar.

◇ Here's a lamb chop that goes nicely—because the lamb is not rare—with white wine. Try it with a full-bodied California Chardonnay, or white Burgundy like Meursault.

TUSCAN LIVER SAUTÉ

1 pound calves' liver, thinly sliced
Salt and black pepper to taste
2 tablespoons olive oil
1 tablespoon butter
1 red onion, sliced very thin
1 clove garlic, minced
1 tablespoon chopped fresh sage
Lemon wedges or balsamic vinegar

Cut off any membranes and, if the liver pieces are thicker than ¼ inch, cut in two crosswise. Season and cut liver in 1-inch strips.

Heat oil and butter and sauté onion, garlic, and sage for 1 or 2 minutes to soften them. Over high heat, add liver and brown quickly, about 1 minute total, to avoid toughening. Serve with lemon wedges or sprinkle with balsamic vinegar.

Chinese Cabbage & Pink Grapefruit Slaw makes a good contrast of flavor and texture.

◆   A slight variation is to sauté the liver in larger pieces and to sprinkle with Italian *gremolata*, or equal parts chopped parsley, garlic, and lemon rind.

◇   Liver can be tough on many wines, but this simple preparation is delicious next to light red Burgundies like Santenay and Mercurey.

HONEY-MUSTARD SPARERIBS

1 side lean spareribs (about 2 pounds)
¼ cup honey
¼ cup Dijon mustard
2 teaspoons soy sauce
2 tablespoons cider vinegar
2 cloves garlic, peeled and mashed
1 fresh red or green chili pepper or Tabasco
    sauce to taste
3 cups sauerkraut, rinsed and drained
1 medium onion, diced
1 cup dry white wine

Trim off excess fat and make a shallow cut between each rib. Drop ribs into a large pot of boiling water and simmer for 40 minutes. Drain well.

Make basting sauce of honey, mustard, soy sauce, vinegar, garlic, and chili by mixing in a blender.

Place sauerkraut, onion, and wine in a shallow baking dish. Lay ribs on top and brush on both sides with sauce, placing ribs fat side up. Roast at 400°F. for 20 minutes, basting until all sauce is used.

To serve, cut between every rib, or every two ribs, and place sauerkraut to the side.

Good with Roast Potato Chips, which you can cook at the same time.

◆　If you have enough time, roast the ribs, without poaching, at 375°F. for about 1½ hours. Cover ribs with basting sauce and cover pan with aluminum foil. Bake 50 minutes with foil on, add sauerkraut, and continue baking ribs uncovered for 30 to 40 minutes more, or until browned.

◇　Simple, fruity reds like young Zinfandels and Barberas are great with sweet 'n' sour ribs.

LAMB WITH
APRICOTS & ALMONDS

1 tablespoon olive oil
1- to 1½-pound-piece boneless lamb (from
      loin or leg)
1 teaspoon black pepper
Salt to taste
½ small onion, minced
½ teaspoon each of ground cumin and
      coriander
¼ teaspoon ground cinnamon
4 to 6 dried apricots, soaked in ½ cup
      boiling water
¼ cup red wine
2 tablespoons almonds, toasted and ground

Put oil in a skillet. Roll lamb in the oil, season meat with pepper and salt. Remove meat and heat skillet until it begins to smoke. Brown lamb well on all sides and remove to a warm serving platter.

In same skillet, sauté onion with spices.

Purée apricots with their liquid and wine in a blender and add to skillet. Scrape in any meat juices and heat through. If sauce is too thick, add a little boiling water.

Slice lamb diagonally, pour sauce over it, and sprinkle with toasted almonds.

Serve with Turnip-Pear Purée or Braised Lemons and Onions.

◆   For a luxury dish, serve the seared lamb in a reduced red wine sauce, similarly spiced and garnished with fresh sliced figs.

◇   Here's another meat dish that is improved more by a white wine than a red wine. The apricot's balance of acid and sweet is a perfect set-up for a Gewürztraminer from Alsace or California.

VENISON WITH
MUSTARD FRUITS

_4 venison noisettes (from the loin), about 1
    pound_
Salt and black and cayenne peppers to taste
2 tablespoons olive oil
⅓ cup currant jelly
2 tablespoons Dijon mustard
1 cup blueberries or blackberries

Season steaks and sauté in oil in hot skillet 3 to 4 minutes a side. Remove to warm platter.

Melt jelly in the same skillet with mustard. Add fruit and simmer just enough to warm it. Pour over venison.

Serve with Apricot Sweet Potatoes and end with Oatmeal-Nut Shortbread and your favorite ice cream.

◆ For a Southern touch, flame the seared noisettes in ¼ cup warmed bourbon and serve with pickled watermelon rind or peach chutney.

◇ Sturdy young red wines bursting with berry fruit are splendid accompaniments to venison. Try a Châteauneuf-du-Pape or a full-bodied California Syrah.

BEEF & WILD
MUSHROOM SAUTÉ

2 beef fillet steaks (1¼ inches thick), about ¾
    pound total
Salt and black pepper to taste
2 tablespoons each of butter and olive oil
½ pound wild mushrooms (shiitake, oyster,
    morel, chanterelle)
2 cloves garlic, minced
2 to 3 sprigs fresh rosemary (or 1 teaspoon dried
    rosemary)

Season fillets and sear in butter and oil in a large skillet, cooking no more than 3 minutes a side for rare beef. Remove to warm platter.

Slice mushrooms and add to the skillet, with garlic and rosemary. Sauté over high heat to brown, and scrape onto the steaks.

Serve with Brie-Arugula Salad with Balsamic Cream Dressing and follow with German Fruit Pancake.

♦ Remember Beef Strogonoff? Cut steaks in ¼-inch slices vertically, season, brown very quickly over high heat, and remove to a platter. Sauté mushrooms and add to the meat. Blend 1 teaspoon tomato paste, ½ teaspoon anchovy paste, and a dash of Worcestershire sauce into ⅔ cup sour cream. Mix with beef and mushrooms and return mixture to skillet to warm for a moment or two.

◊ Aged red Burgundy or Bordeaux, especially from the commune of St. Estèphe in the Médoc, are sure bets with this bosky dish.

VEAL CHOPS WITH PANCETTA & GOAT CHEESE

4 slices pancetta (or prosciutto)
2 to 4 slices goat cheese
2 to 3 fresh sage leaves, chopped
1 clove garlic, minced
Salt and black and cayenne peppers to taste
2 loin veal chops (about 1½ pounds), 1 inch
      thick
Flour
2 tablespoons olive oil
1 tablespoon butter
⅓ cup grated Parmesan cheese

Sauté pancetta 4 or 5 minutes in its own fat, or until it has crisped (or sauté prosciutto in a little olive oil). Remove and chop into slivers. Save fat in skillet.

Mix goat cheese with sage, garlic, and seasonings.

Cut each chop in half horizontally to the bone and spread with goat cheese to make a sandwich. Season chops on both sides and dust with flour.

Heat butter and oil in the pancetta skillet and brown chops over high heat, no more than 3 to 4 minutes a side. Sprinkle chops with Parmesan cheese and run under a broiler to brown cheese. Remove to platter and garnish with chopped pancetta.

Serve with grilled (or broiled) fruits or vegetables and end with Banana Zabaglione.

♦ If you prefer scallopini, sauté pancetta as above, then season scallops, dip in flour, and sauté over high heat with chopped sage. For a different sauce, melt goat cheese in pan with a little wine and pour over scallops.

◇ Serve a light Pinot Noir from Oregon or a young Rosso di Montalcino.

STAR-ANISE BEEF
WITH SNOW PEAS

¾ pound beef fillet
2 tablespoons peanut or vegetable oil
1 tablespoon soy sauce
1 whole star-anise, ground
2 or 3 slices gingerroot, minced
1 clove garlic, minced
1 fresh red chili pepper, seeded and minced
1 tablespoon sherry
1 teaspoon sesame oil
½ cup snow peas

Cut beef into slices ¼ inch thick. Place wok over high heat for about 1 minute. Pour in peanut oil, let heat, and add half the beef strips, stir-frying for about 5 seconds. Remove and repeat with remaining strips. Set strips aside.

Mix remaining ingredients, except for snow peas, add to wok, and stir-fry a few seconds. Add snow peas and stir-fry for 1 minute. Remove from heat, add beef, and turn mixture onto serving platter.

Serve with Honeyed Golden Peppers.

◆　Beef strips are delicious with any number of sauces, including the Poblano Sauce (See Charred Shrimp Poblano) or the Green Sauce (See Wok-Smoked Scallops with Green Sauce) or simply a brandied butter with multicolored peppercorns.

◇　For a solid red wine match, try Beaujolais. If you prefer white wine, consider an Alsatian Pinot Gris.

MISCELLANEOUS

FRESH CORN TAMALE PIE ◆
YOGURT EGGS ◆ GORGONZOLA
RISOTTO ◆ GREEN RICE ◆ RED
LENTILS ◆ TOFU-MISO STIR-FRY
◆ KALE & RED PEPPER SAUTÉ ◆
ONION-CHEESE SOUFFLÉ ◆ HOT
BACON & EGG SALAD ◆ CHINESE
GREENS WITH PESTO ◆ THAI
PAPAYA SALAD ◆ BRIE-ARUGULA
SALAD WITH BALSAMIC CREAM
DRESSING ◆ HOT BEET SALAD ◆
ORANGE-ONION-BASIL SALAD WITH
TAHINI DRESSING ◆ RAW CORN
SALAD WITH CUCUMBER DRESSING

FRESH CORN TAMALE PIE

6 ears fresh corn, kernels cut off (about 6 cups)
Salt and black pepper to taste
1 small onion, chopped
2 cloves garlic, minced
1 tablespoon oil
⅓ pound ground pork
¼ cup raisins
¼ cup stuffed green olives, chopped
2 poblano chilies, roasted, seeded, and chopped
½ teaspoon each of ground cumin and oregano

Purée corn kernels, with salt and pepper, in a blender. Butter a small loaf pan and put half the corn purée in bottom.

Sauté onion and garlic in the oil until softened. Add pork and brown it lightly. Add raisins, olives, chilies, cumin, and oregano and sauté for 2 or 3 minutes.

Spread mixture over bottom layer of corn in loaf pan and cover it with remaining corn purée. Cover pan tightly with foil and bake at 350°F. for about 30 minutes.

Serve with Orange-Onion-Basil Salad with Tahini Dressing and end with Oatmeal-Jam Muffins.

◆ If you lack fresh corn, use 1½ cups cornmeal cooked in ½ cups chicken or beef stock (soften the meal first in ½ cup cold water, then stir in the boiling stock). Cook cornmeal in a double boiler about 10 minutes, stirring often, then pour half into buttered pan, add pork filling, and cover pork with remaining cornmeal. Bake as above.

◇ Try this wine-versatile dish with Blanc de Blancs sparkling wines, light, fruity red wines like Beaujolais, or fruity California Chardonnays.

YOGURT EGGS

2 tablespoons each *olive oil and butter*
4 large eggs
Salt and black pepper to taste
1 cup plain yogurt
2 green onions with tops, chopped, for garnish

Heat oil and butter in a skillet over low heat. Beat eggs with seasonings and add to skillet, stirring slowly in one direction. When they are just set, remove from heat and stir in yogurt. Sprinkle top with green onions.

Serve with toasted pita halves or bagel chips.

♦ Yogurt is also good as a topping for fried eggs, hard- or soft-cooked eggs, or eggs baked in a little butter or cream.

GORGONZOLA RISOTTO

3 to 4 cups chicken stock
1 tablespoon each *of butter and oil*
½ small onion, minced
¾ cup Arborio rice
Salt and white pepper to taste
½ cup white wine
2 ounces Gorgonzola cheese, crumbled
2 tablespoons grated Parmesan cheese
2 tablespoons walnuts, chopped
1 tablespoon half-and-half
1 tablespoon chopped fresh Italian parsley for
*   garnish*

Bring chicken stock to the simmer in a small saucepan and keep covered.

Heat butter and oil in a heavy saucepan and sauté onion for 1 or 2 minutes, to soften. Add rice and stir to coat each grain. Add seasonings and wine and cook slowly until absorbed. Add stock, ½ cup at a time, stirring well each time until liquid is nearly absorbed. When grains are plump and tender but still *al dente* (about 18 to 20 minutes), you don't need more liquid.

Stir in Gorgonzola, Parmesan, walnuts, and half-and-half and mix well, adding a little more stock if desired to make it creamy. Garnish with parsley. Serve immediately.

Serve as a starter or a main dish accompanied by Sautéed Escarole or Wok-Grilled Fennel.

◆   Another classic risotto is based on a mixture of 4 cheeses: Gorgonzola, Fontina, Taleggio, and Parmesan. But almost any cheese, singly or in combination, is delicious. Consider Gruyère, fresh mozzarella, ricotta, mascarpone, goat cheese—you can't go wrong.

◇   Try this dish with a medium-bodied Baròlo or Barbarésco.

GREEN RICE

1 cup basmati rice

SAUCE
1 tablespoon olive oil
1 tablespoon plain yogurt
2 tablespoons each *of chopped fresh parsley and
        cilantro*
1 clove garlic, minced
1 teaspoon lemon juice
½ teaspoon salt
½ teaspoon ground cumin
Black and cayenne peppers to taste

Bring 3 quarts of water (with a tablespoon of salt) to a boil. Rinse rice in a strainer under cold water. Add rice to the boiling water and boil briskly about 7 to 8 minutes (taste a few grains after 6 minutes). Drain rice immediately.

Make sauce by putting ingredients into a blender and puréeing. Toss rice with sauce.

Serve as a companion to fish or shellfish, in general, and to Chinese Shrimp-in-the-Shell in particular.

♦   Rice is much complemented by other sorts of herbs, such as fresh mint leaves, basil, fennel, arugula. To turn the rice above into a one-dish meal, add some sautéed and chopped shrimp or small clams.

RED LENTILS

1 cup red lentils
3 cups chicken stock
½ teaspoon turmeric
3 tablespoons vegetable oil
1 small onion, chopped
2 cloves garlic, minced
1 teaspoon whole cumin seeds
½ teaspoon ground coriander
1 small tomato, seeded and chopped
Salt and cayenne pepper to taste

Pick over lentils to remove any foreign matter and rinse well in a strainer under cold running water. Put lentils in a saucepan and cover with chicken stock. Add turmeric and bring to the simmer. Cover partially with a lid and simmer until soft, 10 to 15 minutes.

Heat oil in a skillet, add onion, garlic, cumin, and coriander and sauté 4 to 5 minutes, or until onions are softened. Add tomato and turn mixture into lentils, mixing well. Taste for seasoning. Serve at room temperature.

For a vegetarian meal, accompany the lentils with Yogurt Eggs or Onion-Cheese Soufflé.

♦ Lentils combine nicely with rice. Use the same seasonings, but add ½ cup cooked rice to the cooked lentils.

TOFU-MISO
STIR-FRY

1 tablespoon miso
½ teaspoon soy sauce
1 tablespoon sherry
3 tablespoons peanut oil
½ pound mushrooms, quartered
2 tablespoons sesame oil
6 green onions with tops, chopped
2 cloves garlic, minced
*1 small fresh red or green chili pepper, seeded
    and minced*
¼ teaspoon ground Szechuan pepper
1 square firm tofu, cubed

Soften miso in soy sauce and sherry and set aside.

Place a wok over high heat, add peanut oil, then mushrooms, and sauté quickly to brown them. Remove mushrooms and set aside.

Add sesame oil to the wok, then onions, garlic, chili, and Szechuan pepper and sauté 2 or 3 minutes.

Add softened miso and tofu and toss tofu gently with the other ingredients. Serve hot or at room temperature.

Serve with Red Lentils or Kale & Red Pepper Sauté.

♦ Stir-fry other chopped vegetables such as carrots, celery, turnips, eggplant, or zucchini, before adding tofu and/or fresh bean sprouts.

◇ This dish is perfect for crisp, off-dry wines like Vouvray Sec and German QbA Riesling.

KALE & RED PEPPER SAUTÉ

1 bunch young kale
1 sweet red pepper
2 tablespoons olive oil
½ red onion, chopped
2 cloves garlic, minced
Salt and cayenne pepper (or red pepper flakes)
    to taste

Wash kale, cut off stems, and chop leaves finely, crosswise.

Seed pepper and cut it in eighths lengthwise, then cut strips diagonally into triangles. Sauté pepper in oil over high heat to char triangles slightly on both sides.

Lower heat and sauté onion and garlic for 2 or 3 minutes.

Add kale and ¼ cup water to the pan. Season, lower heat, and cook, covered, for 8 to 10 minutes, or until kale is tender but still crunchy.

Serve along with the Honey-Mustard Spareribs.

♦ For a one-dish meal, add a handful of young fava or lima beans to the vegetables, together with diced ham or crumbled bacon.

ONION-CHEESE SOUFFLÉ

1 large onion, minced
4 tablespoons butter
½ cup grated Parmesan cheese
⅛ pound Gorgonzola cheese
¼ pound Fontina cheese
3 eggs, separated
Salt and black pepper to taste

Sauté onion gently in 3 tablespoons of the butter about 8 to 10 minutes, until onion is soft and its liquid has evaporated. With remaining butter, grease inside of a baking dish and sprinkle with 2 tablespoons Parmesan.

Crumble Gorgonzola and grate Fontina coarsely into a large bowl. Add onion and half remaining Parmesan.

Beat egg yolks, season them, and add to the onion-cheese mixture. In another bowl, beat egg whites until stiff but not dry. Fold whites gently into the mixture and turn all into baking dish. Sprinkle top with the rest of Parmesan. Bake at 400°F. for 20 to 25 minutes and serve immediately (soufflés sink as they cool).

Serve after Roasted Oysters with Curry Butter or Scallops with Hazelnuts.

♦   Instead of a soufflé, make a gratin by layering onion and cheeses with 2 thin-sliced potatoes and a cup of milk or half-and-half. Bake at 350°F. for 50 to 60 minutes, until potatoes are tender.

◇   Forget the rule about "no wine with eggs" and open up a bottle of light red wine, like Valpolicella or Bardolino.

HOT BACON
& EGG SALAD

2 large eggs
6 thick slices bacon
2 teaspoons balsamic vinegar
Salt and black pepper to taste
1 bunch watercress, arugula, New Zealand
     spinach, escarole, etc.

Cover eggs with cold water in a small pan, bring to the boil, cover, and remove from heat. Let sit for 20 minutes, then run eggs under cold water before peeling.

Fry bacon until crisp, remove, and cut in small pieces. Pour off all but 3 tablespoons of fat. Mix fat with vinegar and seasonings.

Clean greens and put in a salad· bowl. Peel and slice eggs and arrange over the greens. Sprinkle bacon over eggs and pour fat and vinegar mixture over top.

Serve with Chili-Carrot Soup or Smoked Haddock Brandade.

♦ Another version of this salad is to add fried and chopped bacon to 3 beaten eggs, then fry eggs in a tablespoon of fat, turning them once. Turn eggs onto a plate, cut "omelet" in thin slices, and add to greens. Use a bacon-fat dressing as above.

CHINESE GREENS
WITH PESTO

1 small Chinese cabbage
1 small bunch spinach leaves
3 or 4 red radishes

PESTO
⅓ cup basil leaves (packed)
2 tablespoons chopped fresh parsley
1 clove garlic, mashed
¼ cup peanut oil
2 teaspoons sesame oil
1 tablespoon sherry
1 teaspoon soy sauce
Rice wine (optional)

Slice cabbage very thin crosswise, to make 3 or 4 cups.

Wash spinach thoroughly and spin-dry. Bunch leaves and shred finely with a knife or scissors.

Clean and slice radishes. Mix with the spinach and cabbage in a bowl.

Purée ingredients for sauce in a blender. If mixture is too thick, add a little rice wine. Toss sauce with the mixed greens.

A good salad for Pork in Plum Sauce or Duck Breasts with Black Bean Sauce.

◆ Use the same dressing for a salad of chopped bok choy or grilled Japanese eggplant.

THAI PAPAYA SALAD

1 ripe papaya
1 jalapeño pepper, minced
2 ripe tomatoes, seeded and chopped
6 snow peas, cut diagonally in slivers
¼ cup peanut oil
1 to 2 tablespoons lime juice
1 teaspoon brown sugar
½ teaspoon anchovy paste
⅓ cup roasted peanuts, ground

Cut papaya in quarters, peel and remove seeds. Cut in thin slices lengthwise and arrange them on a platter.

Mix jalapeño, tomatoes, and snow peas and sprinkle over papaya.

Combine oil, lime juice, sugar, and anchovy paste, taste for seasoning and adjust. Pour dressing over salad and garnish with peanuts.

Serve with Picadillo or Star-Anise Beef with Snow Peas.

◆ Cut papaya in cubes and toss with shrimp, crisply fried and chopped, and mix with same seasonings.

BRIE-ARUGULA SALAD WITH BALSAMIC CREAM DRESSING

1 bunch arugula
⅓ pound ripe brie

DRESSING
⅓ cup olive oil
½ egg, beaten
1 teaspoon balsamic vinegar
Salt and black pepper to taste

Wash and dry arugula and arrange in a salad bowl.

Cut off rind of cheese and cut cheese in cubes. Mix with arugula.

Purée ingredients for dressing in a blender and pour over salad.

♦ With arugula or other greens, cube brie or other cheeses such as goat cheese, Gruyère, Monterey Jack. Toss cubes in bread crumbs and sauté quickly in olive oil. Add to salad.

HOT BEET SALAD

1 bunch of young beets with tops
½ red onion, sliced thin
4 tablespoons olive oil
1 tablespoon red wine vinegar
Salt and black pepper to taste
¼ cup walnuts, chopped
2 tablespoons chopped fresh mint leaves

Cut off tops 1 inch above beets and boil beets with their skins on in boiling water to cover, about 30 to 45 minutes, or until tender. Drain and run under cold water so that you can slip off their skins. Slice beets thin.

Sauté onion in oil in a small skillet to soften slightly. Remove from heat, then add vinegar, seasonings, walnuts, and mint and pour dressing over beets.

A good salad for the Tuscan Liver Sauté or the Beef & Wild Mushroom Sauté.

♦ For a cold beet salad, try a dressing of sour cream seasoned with lime and fresh dill and sprinkled with walnuts.

ORANGE-ONION-BASIL SALAD WITH TAHINI DRESSING

2 navel oranges
1 medium red or Vidalia onion
2 or 3 radicchio leaves, shredded
6 to 8 fresh basil leaves, shredded

DRESSING
¼ teaspoon soy sauce
Salt and black pepper to taste
1 clove garlic, mashed
2 teaspoons sesame oil
1 tablespoon tahini paste
2 tablespoons orange juice
Lemon juice or vinegar to taste

Peel oranges, remove white pith, and slice thinly. Slice onion very thin and alternate orange and onion slices on a bed of shredded radicchio. Sprinkle with shredded basil leaves.

Combine ingredients for dressing with a fork or small whisk. If mixture is too stiff, add more orange juice or a little white wine. Pour dressing over salad.

Serve with Fresh Corn Tamale Pie.

◆   Use same dressing for salad greens such as endive, slivered Chinese cabbage, or steamed bok choy.

RAW CORN SALAD WITH CUCUMBER DRESSING

4 ears fresh corn, kernels cut off (about 4 cups)
1 sweet red pepper, seeded and chopped
2 large red leaf lettuce leaves

DRESSING
¼ cup seeded and chopped cucumber
1 tablespoon fresh dill
¼ small fresh red or green chili pepper
1 teaspoon lemon juice
1 teaspoon olive oil
⅓ cup plain yogurt
Salt and black pepper to taste

Dill sprigs for garnish

Mix corn and red pepper and place on lettuce leaves.

Purée ingredients for dressing in a blender. Taste for seasoning and adjust. Pour dressing over salad and garnish with a few sprigs of dill.

A good summer salad to go with any grilled fish or fowl.

◆ If raw corn is too raw for you, steam (or grill) the ears for 3 to 4 minutes with their husks on, remove husks, and cut off the kernels. Mix with whatever vegetables you choose.

COMPANIONS

ROAST POTATO CHIPS ◆ APPLED
EGGPLANT ◆ HONEYED GOLDEN
PEPPERS ◆ TURNIP-PEAR
PURÉE ◆ CHINESE CABBAGE &
PINK GRAPEFRUIT SLAW ◆
APRICOT SWEET POTATOES ◆
SAUTÉED ESCAROLE ◆ PESTO
SPAGHETTI SQUASH ◆ TAHINI
BROCCOLI ◆ BRAISED LEMONS &
ONIONS ◆ ONION-BERRY CONFIT
◆ WOK-GRILLED FENNEL

ROAST POTATO CHIPS

2 Idaho potatoes
Salt and black pepper to taste
4 tablespoons olive oil

Scrub potatoes but leave skins on. Slice paper-thin with the slicing disk of a food processor or slice by hand. Season slices quickly and toss with the olive oil in a bowl.

Place slices in a single layer on a baking sheet and bake at 425°F. for 10 to 15 minutes, or until crisped and browned but not burned.

Good by themselves to serve with drinks instead of store-bought potato chips.

◆   Make a fancy potato dish by layering oiled slices in a shallow baking pan, dotting them with a little butter and fresh herbs, such as thyme, and then sprinkling with lemon juice and grated Parmesan cheese. Bake at 400°F. for about 45 to 50 minutes, until potatoes are tender.

APPLED EGGPLANT

1 large Japanese eggplant
1 tart green apple
½ teaspoon salt
¼ teaspoon ground fennel seeds
¼ teaspoon turmeric
⅛ teaspoon cayenne pepper
4 tablespoons vegetable oil

Cut eggplant in ½-inch slices.

Cut apple (leave peel on) in eighths and remove core.

Mix seasonings with a tablespoon of water.

In a skillet, brown apple slices quickly in oil over high heat and remove them. Brown eggplant slices quickly in same oil. Return apples to the skillet, add seasoning, turn heat very low, cover pan, and cook for about 10 minutes, or until the eggplant is tender.

Serve with roast pork or lamb or Turkey Scallopini.

◆   For a variant on the apple-eggplant combo, bake a regular eggplant with a whole cored apple and an onion at 400°F. for about 50 minutes, or until eggplant is soft. Scrape eggplant pulp into a food processor, add apple, salt, and a cup of plain yogurt and purée. Chop onion and add to purée.

HONEYED
GOLDEN PEPPERS

2 sweet golden peppers
2 tablespoons dark honey
1 tablespoon balsamic vinegar
Salt and black pepper to taste
1 tablespoon butter

Stem peppers, cut in half, and remove seeds. Cut each half in strips lengthwise.

Stir honey, vinegar, and seasonings into butter in a skillet and heat. Pour sauce over peppers and serve.

A colorful addition to Pepper Salmon Steaks or a roast bird.

◆ Turn the same ingredients into a sauce for a pork loin or chicken breasts. Simply purée peppers after cooking them in the sauce for about 10 minutes.

TURNIP-PEAR PURÉE

1 large or 2 small turnips
1 ripe pear
2 tablespoons butter
¼ teaspoon mace (or ground nutmeg)
Salt and white and cayenne peppers to taste
Lemon juice to taste
4 to 5 green onions with tops, chopped fine

Peel turnip, cut it in quarters, and drop in boiling water to cook until tender, about 8 to 10 minutes. Drain and put turnip in a food processor.

Cut pear in quarters, remove peel and core, and sauté pear quickly in butter and mace. Put pear in processor with remaining seasonings. Purée until smooth.

Sauté onions for a minute or two and stir into purée.

A delicate companion for Scallops with Hazelnuts or Barbados Chicken.

◆   Turnip-apple is another good combination, especially when the apple is sautéed in a little bacon fat from bacon that you crumble over the top of the purée when done.

CHINESE CABBAGE &
PINK GRAPEFRUIT SLAW

1 small Chinese cabbage
1 pink grapefruit
⅓ cup vinaigrette (or other dressing)

Shred cabbage finely to get 3 or 4 cups. Place in a bowl.

Peel and remove pith of the grapefruit. Segment and remove outer membranes. Place segments on cabbage and pour on vinaigrette or other salad dressing.

This is a very crisp and refreshing accompaniment to a rich dish such as Honey-Mustard Spareribs or Pork in Plum Sauce.

◆ Make a sweet-and-sour slaw of Chinese cabbage by tossing it with vinegar, sugar, minced hot chilies, ginger, and sesame oil.

APRICOT SWEET POTATOES

½ cup dried apricots
¾ cup boiling water
1 large or 2 small sweet potatoes
½ cup plain yogurt or sour cream
Salt and black pepper to taste
Juice of ½ lemon
¼ cup candied ginger, diced

Cover apricots with boiling water and let soak.

Boil sweet potato in its skin for 20 to 30 minutes, or until fork-tender. Cool, peel, and chunk the potato into a processor.

Add apricots and their liquid to the processor, together with yogurt and seasonings, and purée until smooth. Stir in candied ginger or use it for a garnish. ·

Serve with roast venison or turkey or any game.

♦ Other dried fruits, such as apples, currants, or pears, will enhance the inherent sweetness of sweet potatoes; yams or squashes such as acorn or butternut are all good for puréeing.

SAUTÉED ESCAROLE

½ head escarole
1 or 2 cloves garlic, minced
½ small onion, chopped fine
½ jalapeño or other chili pepper, seeded and
       minced
2 tablespoons olive oil
Salt and black pepper to taste

Wash and spin-dry the escarole leaves. Bunch together and cut crosswise into 1-inch segments.

Sauté garlic, onion, and jalapeño in oil in skillet for 1 or 2 minutes. Add escarole and seasonings and sauté about 5 minutes or until escarole is somewhat wilted.

Serve as a companion for Roasted Garlic Cod or Steamed Clams with Vegetables.

◆   Sautéed escarole is a fine bitter accent for pasta in the same way that broccoli rabe is. As a green, escarole would also substitute well for the rabe in Squab & Rabe.

PESTO
SPAGHETTI SQUASH

$\frac{1}{2}$ *spaghetti squash, cut lengthwise*
2 tablespoons olive oil

YOGURT-PESTO
2 tablespoons olive oil
$\frac{1}{3}$ cup plain yogurt
$\frac{2}{3}$ cup basil leaves, packed
3 tablespoons chopped fresh parsley
$\frac{1}{2}$ teaspoon salt
1 large clove garlic, mashed
2 tablespoons pine nuts, toasted
2 tablespoons grated Parmesan cheese

Remove seeds from cut squash, brush flat surface with olive oil and place cut-side down in baking pan. Bake at 400°F. for 40 to 50 minutes, or until fork-tender.

Put all the ingredients for pesto, except cheese, into a blender and purée until smooth. If mixture is too thick, add boiling water or chicken stock. Remove sauce to a bowl and stir in cheese.

With a fork, shred squash into spaghetti-like strands and pour pesto over top.

This can be a meal in itself, like pasta and pesto, or can be a fit companion for a soup or a stir-fry.

♦ This comically versatile squash is also delicious with a Poblano Sauce (see Charred Shrimp Poblano) or pumpkin-seed sauce (see Pumpkin-Seed Quail). Or, treat it like a real pasta and toss it with clams, garlic, and parsley or a *gremolata* of grated lemon rind, garlic, and parsley.

TAHINI BROCCOLI

1 pound broccoli
1 tablespoon olive oil
1 tablespoon tahini
2 tablespoons boiling water
1 tablespoon lemon juice
Salt and black pepper to taste

Cut off tough ends of broccoli stems and remove outer leaves. Cut off flowerets with their stems and peel off any tough skin from stems.

Drop broccoli into boiling salted water and boil for about 3 minutes, or until just tender. Drain.

Put oil and tahini in a bowl and pour on boiling water, stirring until mixture is smooth. Add lemon juice and seasoning. Pour sauce on a plate and arrange broccoli on top.

Good for a Beef & Wild Mushroom Sauté or Onion-Cheese Soufflé.

◆ For a broccoli purée, proceed as above, only purée the boiled broccoli with the tahini and seasonings in a food processor. A tahini dressing also does well with broccoli rabe or other bitter greens, such as mustard, kale, or collards.

BRAISED LEMONS
& ONIONS

1 lemon
1 large onion, such as Vidalia
2 tablespoons butter or olive oil
⅓ cup dry vermouth
*⅛ teaspoon each of ground cinnamon and black
    pepper*

Slice lemon, skin on, as thinly as possible. Remove any seeds.

Peel and slice onion as thinly as possible.

Put lemon and onion in a skillet with the remaining ingredients, cover pan, and simmer for 8 to 10 minutes.

This is a sharp palate perker to accompany roast duck or goose or pork.

◆ If you prefer a sweet-sour taste, simply add a tablespoon of honey to the skillet with the other ingredients.

ONION-BERRY
CONFIT

1 tablespoon butter
1 large yellow onion, diced
1 tablespoon honey
1 tablespoon Campari
1 to 2 tablespoons lemon juice
1 cup blueberries or other fresh berries

Heat butter in skillet and brown onion over high heat, stirring frequently, for 3 or 4 minutes. Add honey and caramelize for 2 or 3 more minutes. Remove from heat, add Campari, lemon juice, and berries and mix well.

A good garnish for duck, turkey, pork, game, and other meats.

◆ For a sweeter taste, use crème de cassis instead of Campari. For a thicker sauce, purée a quarter of the caramelized onion with the flavorings before adding the fruit.

WOK-GRILLED
FENNEL

1 head fennel
2 tablespoons olive oil
1 teaspoon balsamic vinegar

Cut a thin slice off root end of fennel and cut off top stalks. Cut head in half lengthwise and then in ½-inch slices lengthwise.

Heat wok until almost smoking, add oil and then fennel. Char slices on both sides, turning frequently. Sprinkle with vinegar and serve hot or at room temperature.

Fennel goes especially well with fish and chicken.

◆   For a one-dish meal, grill fennel with strips of sweet red pepper or chili poblano, red onions, zucchini, and eggplant. Mix with black Mediterranean olives and strips of seared tuna or swordfish.

AFTERWARDS

CHOCOLATE-CHILI CREAM ◆
PERNOD PEARS ◆ OATMEAL-JAM
MUFFINS ◆ GRAPE FREEZIES ◆
GINGERED FIGS ◆ BANANA
ZABAGLIONE ◆ VANILLA ICE
CREAM WITH WHITE-CHOCOLATE
RASPBERRY SAUCE ◆ DRIED
APRICOT FOOL ◆ GERMAN FRUIT
PANCAKE ◆ JALAPEÑO-LIME ICE
◆ PLUM MASCARPONE TART WITH
QUICK NUT CRUST ◆ BRANDY
ALEXANDER PARFAIT ◆ OATMEAL-
NUT SHORTBREAD ◆ HOT MINT-
JULEP PEACHES ◆ CHILI ORANGES

CHOCOLATE-
CHILI CREAM

2 ounces bittersweet chocolate of high quality
2 tablespoons espresso coffee, brewed very
strong
¼ cup heavy cream
1 teaspoon pure ground chili
2 tablespoons skinned hazelnuts, chopped

Melt chocolate slowly with coffee, cream, and chili over a very low flame, stirring as needed. Simmer to thicken slightly, about 10 minutes.

Pour mixture into 2 small pots-de-crème cups or small bowls and chill for at least 30 minutes. Sprinkle tops with the hazelnuts.

Serve instead of chocolate truffles with coffee after a meal of splendor.

◆   Mexico has put chocolate, coffee, and chili together for a couple of thousand years and the combination does wonders for cookies and cakes as well as sauces. For a sauce, mix proportions above with 1 cup crème fraîche and cover with fresh raspberries.

PERNOD PEARS

2 *ripe pears*
2 *tablespoons unsalted pistachio nuts, chopped*
    coarsely
2 *tablespoons Pernod*

Halve pears, peel, remove core, and place pears cavity side up on a square of tin foil. Fill each cavity with nuts and pour Pernod over top. Bring foil up around pears and seal edges tightly. Bake at 400°F. for 30 minutes. Serve hot, warm, or cold.

Refreshingly light after a hearty meal.

♦   Instead of pistachios, fill the cavities with candied ginger and use Kirsch or, if you're feeling extravagant, the pear brandy called Poire.

◇   Delicious next to a glass of late-harvest California or Australian Riesling.

OATMEAL-JAM MUFFINS

4 tablespoons butter
1 egg, beaten
1 cup buttermilk
½ cup rolled oats
1½ cups all-purpose flour
¼ cup sugar
1 tablespoon baking powder
½ teaspoon baking soda
½ teaspoon salt
½ cup walnuts, chopped
⅓ cup raspberry jam

Preheat the oven to 375°F.

Melt butter in small pan. Use a small amount of it to butter a muffin tin. Mix rest of butter with egg, buttermilk, and rolled oats. Let mixture sit for 5 minutes.

Mix the remaining dry ingredients together, add nuts, and combine with liquid mixture.

Fill muffin cups two-thirds full with the batter. Make a well in the middle of each muffin with your finger and add a large teaspoon of jam. Bake for about 20 to 25 minutes. Makes a dozen muffins. Freeze what you don't eat.

Muffins for dessert is a good ploy for health zanies who are convinced that muffins are good for you but sweets are not.

♦   If you are heavily into bran or oat bran, substitute it for oatmeal and add raisins to the nuts.

GRAPE FREEZIES

1 bunch red seedless grapes
½ cup confectioners' sugar

Put grapes in freezer for about 30 minutes. Take out, sift sugar over them, and serve. The grapes should be very cold but not frozen.

For a pretty dessert centerpiece, surround grapes with slices of Chinese star-fruit, sometimes called carombola, dipped in sugar.

♦ For a grape ice, purée fresh seedless grapes in a blender with grape juice, lemon juice, and sugar syrup. Freeze as quickly as possible.

AFTERWARDS

GINGERED FIGS

1 cup dried figs
¼ cup candied ginger, chopped
2 tablespoons sugar
Juice of ½ lemon
1 cup boiling water
¼ cup walnuts, chopped

Put figs in saucepan with ginger. Mix sugar, lemon juice, and water and pour over figs. Cover pan and simmer gently for 20 to 30 minutes until figs are plump and tender. Put figs in a bowl, sprinkle with nuts, and serve warm or chilled.

Think of this as a fruit dessert with a little extra zap.

♦   Try a mixture of chopped figs, dates, and prunes, simmered the same way, and served with yogurt mixed with nuts and honey.

◇   Late-harvest Gewürztraminers from California are fine accompaniments to simple fig-based desserts.

BANANA ZABAGLIONE

3 egg yolks
3 tablespoons sugar
⅓ cup Marsala
1 banana
1 teaspoon fresh lemon juice
2 amaretti biscuits, crushed, for garnish

Mix egg yolks with sugar and beat with a whisk or an electric egg beater in top part of double boiler, over boiling water. When mixture becomes light and fluffy, add Marsala a little at a time and beat strenuously until all absorbed.

Slice banana, divide slices between two glass bowls, and sprinkle lemon juice over slices. Pour zabaglione over bananas and sprinkle with crushed amaretti. Serve hot or cold.

A good Italianate ending to a dinner of pasta and salad.

♦   Instead of Marsala, beat in another sweet dessert wine such as Essencia (made of orange muscat grapes), tokay, or sauternes, and serve over sliced peaches or nectarines.

◇   Great with a chilled glass of Marsala, or whatever sweet wine is used in the preparation.

VANILLA ICE CREAM WITH WHITE-CHOCOLATE RASPBERRY SAUCE

1 pint fresh raspberries
¼ pound white chocolate
½ cup heavy cream
¼ cup honey
¾ pint vanilla ice cream

Purée raspberries in blender and sieve to remove seeds.

Melt chocolate with heavy cream and honey over low heat, stirring until chocolate dissolves. Simmer mixture until it thickens slightly, 2 or 3 minutes. Remove from heat and let cool for 5 minutes.

Pour chocolate sauce and raspberry purée in swirls over ice cream.

Not for every day, maybe, but on the other hand, why not?

♦   Use the same sauce to cover fresh fruit or to cloak a meringue glacé.

DRIED APRICOT FOOL

½ cup dried apricots
1 to 2 tablespoons lemon juice
2 tablespoons apricot jam
1 tablespoon almond liqueur (see Note)
½ cup heavy cream, whipped

Cover apricots with water in a small saucepan, bring to boil, and simmer for 10 minutes. Drain but reserve liquid.

Purée apricots in a food processor with lemon juice, jam, and liqueur. If more liquid is needed, add enough apricot liquid to make a thick purée.

Whip cream and fold into fruit mixture. Pile mixture into glass bowls.

Serve with Oatmeal-Nut Shortbread.

◆   Turn mixture into a frozen soufflé by beating 2 egg whites until foamy, then gradually adding ¼ confectioners' sugar until whites are stiff but not dry. Fold in the apricot purée with its flavorings and the whipped cream, turn it into a mold, and freeze.

NOTE: You can substitute ½ teaspoon almond flavoring, plus 1 teaspoon or more Kirsch.

GERMAN FRUIT PANCAKE

2 eggs
½ cup milk
½ cup all-purpose flour
1 teaspoon sugar
⅛ teaspoon salt
3 tablespoons butter
½ cup orange marmalade

Put eggs, milk, flour, sugar, and salt in a blender and blend until smooth.

Melt butter in an 8-inch-wide heavy skillet in oven heated to 425°F. When skillet is hot, pour in batter and return pan to oven. Bake for 10 to 15 minutes, until pancake is puffed and browned.

Spread pancake with marmalade, cut it into quarters, and serve like a pizza.

This is a lazy man's popover to cover with any kind of jam.

◆ Turn a German pancake into a French *clafouti* by pouring batter over 2 cups chopped fresh fruit, such as apples, peaches, or berries mixed with fruit preserves. Bake in a hot skillet as above.

JALAPEÑO-LIME ICE

1 cup sugar
3 jalapeño peppers, seeded and minced
1½ cups water
Rind and juice of 2 to 3 limes (½ cup juice)

Put sugar and peppers in saucepan with the water and heat, stirring, until sugar is dissolved. Cool quickly in the refrigerator. Add lime, taste thoroughly for the exact degree of sweet, sour, and hot that you want, remembering that freezing will diminish flavor. Freeze mixture in metal tray or bowl.

This makes a refreshing ice between courses, as well as a dessert.

◆ Use orange juice instead of lime, substituting 2 cups juice and pulp (free of membranes), plus orange rind.

PLUM MASCARPONE TART WITH QUICK NUT CRUST

CRUST
2 cups walnuts
1 tablespoon brown sugar
1 egg white, beaten

FILLING
1 pound Italian purple plums
½ cup plum jam or blueberry preserves
Rind and juice of 1 lemon
¼ cup Port
⅓ cup hazelnuts, toasted and ground
½ pound mascarpone
½ cup sour cream

To make crust, toast walnuts for about 8 to 10 minutes over low heat in skillet, then grind nuts in food processor. Mix with sugar and beat in egg white. Press mixture evenly into a 9-inch pie pan and bake at 300°F. for 10 to 15 minutes, until lightly browned.

Remove pits from plums and put plums in food processor with jam, lemon, and Port. Pulse several times to make a chunky purée. Taste for sweetness and add more jam if desired.

Sprinkle half the hazelnuts over the baked crust and spoon in the purée to make an even layer. Beat mascarpone with sour cream and cover plums with white swirls. Sprinkle top with remaining nuts.

A very showy conclusion to a grand or simple meal.

◆   Almost any fresh fruits can be treated this way, according to the season. Think of chunked peaches with peach jam, apricots with apricot jam, strawberries with strawberry jam, etc.

◇   Try a late-harvest Zinfandel or young Ruby Port.

BRANDY ALEXANDER PARFAIT

¾ pint vanilla ice cream
3 tablespoons crème de cacao
3 tablespoons brandy
¼ cup heavy cream
¼ cup hazelnuts, toasted and ground

Scoop ice cream into 2 parfait glasses. Pour crème de cacao, brandy, and cream into blender and whip until slightly thickened. Pour mixture over ice cream and top with toasted hazelnuts.

Good for when you want a little something extra.

♦ Make a delicious frozen Brandy Alexander. Chop up the hazelnuts in a food processor. Then add the rest of the ingredients and purée. Freeze the mixture, puréeing it quickly again just before serving.

OATMEAL-NUT SHORTBREAD

¼ *pound (1 stick) butter*
⅓ *cup brown sugar*
½ *cup all-purpose flour*
⅛ *teaspoon salt*
⅓ *cup rolled oats*
½ *teaspoon vanilla*
½ *cup walnuts or pecans, chopped*
Ground cinnamon and granulated sugar for
the top

Cream butter and sugar until fluffy, or pulse in food processor until smooth. Mix flour, salt, oats, and vanilla and mix lightly with butter-sugar mixture, or pulse in processor until just mixed (as in making pastry dough). Add nuts and mix well.

Press dough with your fingertips into an 8- or 9-inch pie pan, and with a sharp knife mark top into 8 or 12 pieces. Sprinkle top with cinnamon and granulated sugar. Bake at 300°F. for about 25 minutes, until lightly browned. Cut pieces all the way through and let cool in pan.

A nice companion for fruit sherbets or fresh fruit and an essential for afternoon tea.

◆   For a savory instead of a sweet shortbread, omit sugar and vanilla and mix butter, flour, oats, and nuts with salt, cumin, lots of black pepper, and ¼ cup grated Cheddar cheese.

HOT MINT-
JULEP PEACHES

2 ripe peaches
1 tablespoon butter
1 tablespoon sugar
2 tablespoons bourbon
¼ cup chopped fresh mint leaves

Peel and slice peaches. Heat butter until bubbly in a skillet over high heat. Add peaches and remaining ingredients. Turn fruit gently just to warm it through. Serve hot or at room temperature.

This is a fine summer dessert to serve cold, but if you chill it, add another tablespoon of sugar with a teaspoon of lime juice to prevent peaches from turning brown.

♦   Flavor your peaches this way when making a peach shortcake, covered with whipped cream.

◇   A festive ending to a meal, especially when served with a light sparkling Moscato d'Asti.

CHILI ORANGES

2 navel (or blood) oranges
1 teaspoon pure ground chili (mild)
¼ teaspoon salt
Sprigs of fresh cilantro for garnish

Peel oranges, remove pith, and slice thin.
Mix chili and salt and sprinkle mixture over oranges. Garnish with cilantro sprigs.

A real palate cleanser at the end of a rich meal.

◆ Try the orange-chili combination in a sorbet, puréeing orange pulp with extra orange juice, adding a sugar syrup (or orange marmalade) to chili, and freezing.

◇ Try a wine made from orange muscat, like Essencia.

INDEX